Y

THIS INDENTURE, made the **30th** day of August, in the year one thousand nine hundred and nineteen, by and between HENRY E. HUNTINGTON, of the City of San Marino, County of Los Angeles, State of California, party of the first part, and HOWARD E. HUNTINGTON, ARCHER MILTON HUNTINGTON, W. E. DUNN, GEORGE S. PATTON and GEORGE E. HALE, parties of the second part, witnesseth:

WHEREAS, said Henry E. Huntington desires, in his lifetime, to promote and advance learning, the arts and sciences, and to promote the public welfare by founding, endowing and having maintained a library, art gallery, museum and park within this state;

NOW, THEREFORE, to that end, and for such purposes, and acting in pursuance of an act of the legislature of the State of California, hereinafter mentioned, the said party of the first part, in consideration of the premises and the sum of Five ($5.00) Dollars, lawful money of the United States to him in hand paid by the parties of the second part, the receipt whereof is hereby acknowledged, does hereby convey and release unto the said parties of the second part, and to their successors, the following described property belonging to the said Henry E. Huntington, and situated and being within the State of California, to-wit:-

NINET
EENN
INET
EE
N

NINETEEN NINETEEN

James Glisson and Jennifer A. Watts

The Huntington Library,
Art Collections, and Botanical Gardens
San Marino, California

Contents

Foreword

To celebrate The Huntington's first one hundred years, our centennial exhibition takes an unconventional approach. Instead of surveying an entire century, it shines a light on just one year: the institution's first, 1919. This year was immensely consequential, both personally for the Huntingtons—with Henry and Arabella signing the formal trust indenture that established the Henry E. Huntington Library and Art Gallery—and globally, as millions of soldiers returned from the Great War, and Europe attempted to emerge from the nightmare of destruction.

Curators James Glisson and Jennifer A. Watts have chosen to structure the exhibition in congruent parts: objects from and about 1919 offer both texture and context to the institution's beginnings. Every item in the show comes from The Huntington's remarkable collections. Included in this inventory are maps, photos, art, and botanical specimens, even Henry Huntington's business records and invoices from this foundational year. A view of Henry the book collector also emerges through a few prized highlights that the founder chose to display to an august gathering of New York Authors Club members in December 1919. In focusing on a momentous year in this way, our curators create a portrait of the Huntingtons woven into the tapestry of national and international events.

As a new president, I am delighted to be joining and celebrating The Huntington as it looks back on its extraordinary first century and forward to its second. When Jenny and James described to me their idea to launch our centennial with a focus on a single year in the life of the Huntingtons, I was reminded of the temporal constraint that James Joyce adopted in composing *Ulysses*, the modern Irish epic that he was serially publishing in 1919. *Ulysses* is perhaps the most famous example of a circadian novel, a quintessentially modernist form that depicts its main characters by concentrating on one day—in this case, June 16, 1904. The novel records the physical and mental furniture of Leopold and Molly Bloom, their memories and dreams as well as their material possessions, down to an inventory of the books in Leopold's library and the invoices stacked in his drawer. In recording a day in the lives of his characters, Joyce enmeshes them in a social, material, and historical web. Through his strict temporal focus on these Dubliners, Joyce paradoxically presents one of the most encompassing pictures of the modern world. Fittingly, issues of *The Little Review* in which chapters of *Ulysses* were published, along with a number of first editions of the novel, are now part of The Huntington's collections.

Through a similar temporal constraint, our curators pair very personal portraits of the Huntingtons with the tumultuous social and political landscape in which their legacy took shape. They tell a story at once local, national, and international: an American couple who transferred European cultural patrimony to America and then moved it again from New York to their new home in San Marino, California. The exhibition contains a selection of the rare, signature items that have given The Huntington its reputation as a national treasure. But it includes many surprises as well, lesser-known items that tell other stories that exceed Henry Huntington's vision.

The extraordinary institution the Huntingtons founded in August 1919 helped to fulfill Henry's vision of a future in which "the Pacific Coast will one day be the center of culture extending around the world." But our centennial celebration also prods us to revisit how Henry's vision of the future is challenged by the radical demographic transformation of this state and this country. As The Huntington moves into its second century, we are working to create new narratives for a different moment in our national life. We are excited to address this challenge, both by building partnerships and by inviting artists, writers, scholars, and students to reinterpret our collections, augmenting and altering them through new lenses.

Karen R. Lawrence, *President*
The Huntington Library, Art Collections,
and Botanical Gardens

THE HUNTINGTON

PREVIOUS SPREAD
(clockwise from left)
Harold A. Parker, *Orderlies and a Patient during Influenza Outbreak, Wilson Middle School, Pasadena*, 1919

C. C. Pierce, *Interior of St-Gervais-et-St-Protais, Paris*, 1919

"Some War Cross Winners of 8th Illinois (370th Infantry)"

Mount Wilson Observatory, *G58 M8, N.G.C. 6523, "Sagittarius," Irregular Nebula, Exposure 3 hrs., 60-inch Reflector*, June 27, 1919

William F. Hertrich, *Construction of the Library Building, Looking Southeast, Showing the West Wing*, December 19, 1919

J. C. Milligan, *Crowd outside Bullock's Department Store for August Clearance Sale, Los Angeles*, 1919

FOLLOWING SPREAD
Road to the Huntington Residence through the Citrus Orchard, San Marino, ca. 1919

Alfonso C. Gomez, Henry E. Huntington's longtime valet, sat for an interview in 1959, more than three decades after his employer's death. At sixty-six years old, the Spanish-born "Gomez," as the Huntingtons called him, held a storehouse of personal and institutional memories. He had spent more time with Mr. Huntington in his final decade than anyone else, and formalities between the two had eased.

Gomez told a nostalgic story about an afternoon's meandering walk with Henry and Arabella through their San Marino ranch. The couple strolled north from their mansion while Gomez kept an eye on Buster, Mrs. Huntington's ill-mannered dog. After some distance, Arabella, nearly blind and walking with difficulty, stopped and spoke to her spouse. "You know, we are doing so much," Arabella said. "I hope you will live many years yet, and I hope to live many years yet, but we are talking so much about it. We have got to make a decision where we want to be buried." She put her foot on a spot, the highest point of their property, and asked Gomez to mark it. Henry Huntington said little. Their final resting place had been decided then and there, by an infirm, elderly woman's footprint on a Southern California knoll.

That fateful walk took place in 1919. A world-shattering war, one that novelist John Dos Passos later described as a "blast that blew out all the Diogenes lanterns," had just ended. As millions of soldiers and volunteers returned home, war's aftershocks reverberated on other fronts: labor riots, racial-terror lynchings, and protest marches roiled the streets and countryside. At the Paris Peace Conference, President Woodrow Wilson and Allied heads of state carved up empires in Eastern Europe and the Middle East, adopting a punitive stance toward Germany in hopes of mapping a postwar world of enduring peace. On the other side of the globe in California, one of America's wealthiest couples faced their own mortality and looked to the future by safeguarding the past.

A Founder and a Year

ABOVE
Henry E. Huntington on a Garden Path at His San Marino Ranch (detail), 1918, glass plate negative, 8 x 10 in.

FACING
U.S. Army Signal Corps, *Aerial Photograph of the Huntington Ranch* (detail), ca. 1919, gelatin silver print, 6 x 5 ¼ in.

January 29, 1919— U.S. Congress ratifies Eighteenth Amendment, prohibiting "the manufacture, sale, or transportation" of alcohol.

June 28, 1919— Treaty of Versailles is signed at the Paris Peace Conference, ending World War I.

11

Having made one decision about eternity, Arabella and Henry Huntington made a second one official. On August 30, 1919, they signed a legal document bequeathing the gardens, books, and art collections to the public, "to advance learning in the arts and sciences." The trust formalized an arrangement Henry had been cannily plotting for years. The establishment of the Henry E. Huntington Library and Art Gallery, on the grounds the founders had chosen for their eternal rest, would prove to be a monumental, even death-defying, act.

Once the plan was announced, reporters and others began to inquire about an autobiography describing his career. Huntington demurred. "This Library will tell the story," he replied. "It represents the reward of all the work that I have ever done and the realization of much happiness."

When considering a centennial exhibition, we decided to take Henry Huntington at his word. Rather than offer a narrow account of the collector and philanthropist, we chose to look outward to the nation and the world. Would it be possible, we wondered, to narrate 1919 by mining the millions of documents, objects, paintings, ephemera, photographs, and volumes found in The Huntington's archives, galleries, and book stacks? We examined the institution's founding and founders through the lens of a single cataclysmic year.

Nineteen Nineteen, the exhibition and this accompanying book, draws exclusively from The Huntington's collections. The year and the actions of the institution's founders are organized according to five themes— *Fight, Return, Map, Move,* and *Build*—verbs the Huntingtons lived and embraced. An additional section, *Portraits*, highlights personalities and lesser-known aspects of institutional history and memory.

August 18, 1919— Construction begins on the Huntington Library building designed by Myron Hunt.

Arabella Huntington Traveling in Europe (detail), ca. 1898. Courtesy of The Hispanic Society of America, New York

Henry Huntington traveled by private train to Philadelphia to undergo surgery in 1927. Gomez was by his side. It had been eight years since he and Arabella had signed the founding trust indenture, and three long years since her death. Huntington wanted the operation over and done. He longed to get back to California quickly. He was eager to build a cozy cottage, a tucked-away place where he could observe people enjoying the mansion, the library exhibits, and the gardens and grounds. "He said it so many times," Gomez remembered. The giver was eager to see the response to his gift.

Huntington returned to San Marino in that same railroad car, the shades drawn in mourning to mark his death. He was eventually laid to rest next to his beloved Belle at the agreed-upon spot. A century later, his hope that their creation—an Edenic botanical garden and a superb collection of books and art—would outlive and honor them has exceeded his dreams.

James Glisson
Interim Chief Curator of American Art

Jennifer A. Watts
Curator of Photography and Visual Culture

ABOVE
George H. Kahn, *Henry E. Huntington with a Grandchild,* ca. August 1916, gelatin silver print, 7 ½ x 5 ½ in.

FOLLOWING SPREAD
"Drafted Men Crossing the East River to Take the Train to Camp Upton, Yaphank," in *The War of the Nations,* 1919, rotogravure, New York Times

1919 ———— Fight

Act quickly! The revolution
obliges. Its hours count as
months, its days as years,
in world history.

—Rosa Luxemburg,
Die Rote Fahne (The Red Flag),
January 7, 1919

Pasadena Snorts under Flu
Masks: Sixty Violators
of the New Flu Law
Are Arrested
First Day

—*Los Angeles Times*,
January 21, 1919

We return. We return from fighting.
We return fighting. Make way
for Democracy! We saved
it in France, and by the
Great Jehovah, we will
save it in the United
States of America,
or know the
reason
why.

—W. E. B. Du Bois,
"Returning Soldiers,"
The Crisis, May 1919

FACING
C. C. Pierce, *Interior of St-Gervais-et-
St-Protais, Paris*, 1919, gelatin silver
print, 6 ½ x 4 ¾ in.

INSERT
(front) *Henry E. Huntington at
Dedication Ceremony of the Southern
Pacific Railroad, Ogden-Lucin Cut-Off,
Utah* (detail), November 26, 1903,
gelatin silver print, 7 ½ x 9 ½ in.;
(back) *Belle D. Worsham and Archer M.
Worsham* (detail), ca. 1871. Courtesy
of The Hispanic Society of America,
New York

FOLLOWING SPREAD
"Birdseye View of Ypres," in
The War of the Nations

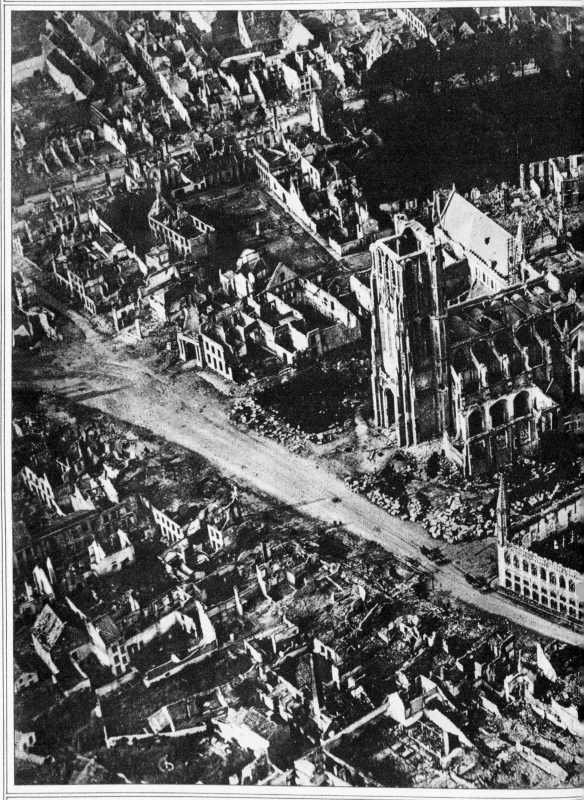

HOUSES WITHOUT ROOFS, ROOMS WITHOUT WINDOWS, WALLS WITHOUT SU

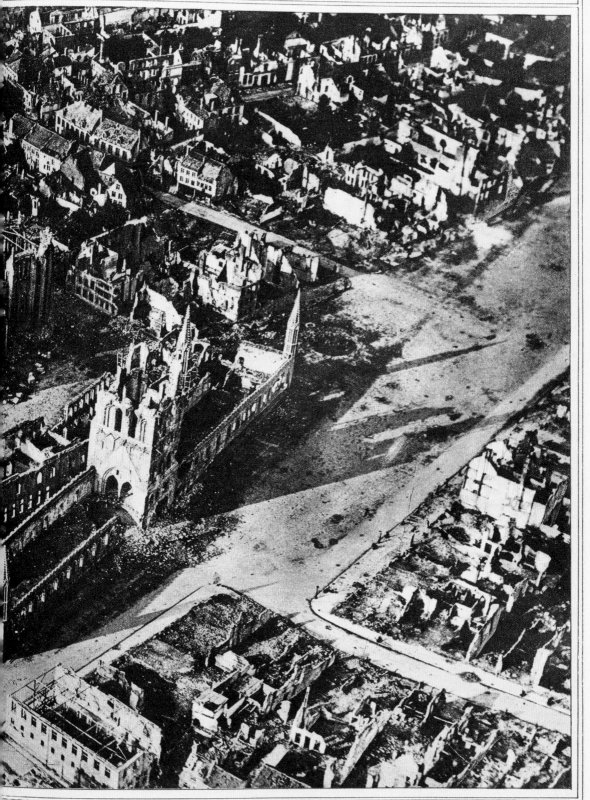

TERY THAT ONCE WAS A CITY—YPRES, AFTER THE GERMAN INVASION.

Breuer, *Vergesst uns Gefangene nicht* (Don't Forget Us Prisoners of
War), 1919, lithograph, 28 x 37 ⅜ in., Volksbund zum Schutze
der deutschen Kriegs- und Zivilgefangenen (German
Welfare Organization for War and Civilian Prisoners),
Kunstanstalt Carl Sabo, Berlin, Germany

Violence begets violence. One fight inexorably leads to another. So it was with the spark that unleashed the firestorm of the Great War. On June 28, 1914, a group of Serbian nationalists in Austrian-occupied Sarajevo assassinated Archduke Franz Ferdinand. In retaliation, Austria-Hungary invaded Serbia, toppling the dominoes of long-nursed ethnic rivalries and grievances among nations. By autumn, the French, British, and Russian troops of the Allied Powers were facing off against soldiers of the German Empire, Austria-Hungary, and the Ottoman Empire—the Central Powers. On the plains of northern France and Belgium, armies settled into the stalemate of trench warfare, the possibility of a quick, decisive defeat mired in the mud.

The scale of the killing shocked the world. Historians estimate that between 8 and 10 million people died on both sides. The French lost 1.3 million, and the Germans 2 million. When dry statistics could not suffice, metaphor and symbol stepped in. A bird's-eye view of Ypres, Belgium, published by the *New York Times* in 1919, reveals the skeletons of the city's famed Cloth Hall and Saint Martin's Cathedral (pp. 22–23). The caption mourns "the ghastly ruin of that once flourishing city." By war's end, Ypres and its environs had seen five battles, including the infamously gruesome Battle of Passchendaele, with at least 400,000 casualties. Ypres was "a cemetery that was once a city."

As if the scale were not enough, the most advanced technology available, the fruit of the Scientific and Industrial Revolutions, was mobilized to kill and destroy with diabolical creativity. While machine guns and airplanes multiplied the terrors of war, poison gas choked and maimed; even a century later, its use is condemned as barbaric. When American artist John Singer Sargent visited Arras, France, he sketched blinded victims of mustard gas attacks who were leaning on each other (p. 38). In his drawing, the thrice-repeated outstretched

February 6, 1919—Seattle General Strike begins when 60,000 workers protest the continuation of wage controls instituted during the war.

April 13, 1919—Socialist Eugene V. Debs begins a ten-year prison sentence for a fiery 1918 antiwar speech he gave in Ohio.

July 27, 1919—
The murder of black teenager Eugene Williams at a Chicago beach sparks the Chicago Race Riots; 6,500 state militia troops are mobilized to restore order.

arm gropes for support in the darkness and epitomizes the ghastly effects of the burns and blisters on eyes and skin. Improved gas masks made the gases less fatal (pp. 48–49) but did nothing for those already disfigured.

America's entry into the war in April 1917 helped turn the tide for the Allies, as over two million American soldiers crossed the Atlantic. Just as debilitating for the Central Powers was the British naval blockade. By the fall of 1918, the German Empire faced the inevitability of defeat and internal collapse, with mutinies, revolutions, and economic desperation. The armistice that ended hostilities between the Central Powers and the Allies went into effect at eleven in the morning Central European Time on November 11, 1918. An audio recording captured the moment the booming guns flatlined after four years, giving the illusion of a clean break, a before and after (pp. 52–53). But could it be so simple? Stopping the war machine was the easy part. A generation had been mowed down. The monarchies of Germany, Austria-Hungary, and Russia had vanished. Their shards lay on the ground, waiting for diplomats to glue various ethnic minorities into new nations and forge a durable peace.

November 1, 1919—
400,000 U.S. miners join a mass coal strike, which ends in December and results in higher wages for workers.

Violence begets violence. One fight inexorably leads to another. The year began inauspiciously. The German kaiser abdicated two days before the armistice, and a revolutionary parliament convened in Berlin. In January 1919, the newly formed Communist Party of Germany led a short-lived uprising under Rosa Luxemburg and Karl Liebknecht, who were assassinated on January 15. Days later, Germans elected a parliament to draft the ill-fated Weimar Constitution. Printed posters and pamphlets—issued by successive governments, volunteer organizations, and political parties, whether Communist, Social Democrat, or Catholic—told people how to get help with utilities, how to assist prisoners of war, and which zones of Berlin to avoid because of armed troops (pp. 36–37).

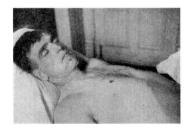

Postmortem Photograph of John Looney, in Walker C. Smith, *The Everett Massacre*, ca. 1919, Industrial Workers of the World, Chicago

CLOCKWISE FROM TOP
*Influenza Epidemic in Pasadena,
California,* 1919, gelatin
silver prints, 3 ½ x 5 ¹¹⁄₁₆ in.,
4 ⅝ x 2 ⅞ in., 4 ½ x 3 ½ in.

27

Amid war, revolution, and unrest, the third wave of an H1N1 influenza pandemic peaked in the winter of 1918–19, killing millions around the world. In Pasadena, a proactive city council passed an unpopular ordinance threatening arrest to anyone who did not wear a mask in public, and the Red Cross opened an infirmary at a local middle school.

Pent-up grievances exploded throughout the United States, owing in part to a cripplingly high rate of inflation, running at nearly 60 percent between January 1914 and January 1919. This vastly eroded purchasing power. Some labor organizations, like the Industrial Workers of the World, or I.W.W., had taken an unpopular antiwar stance and fought for unionization during the war and after. The red-ink bloodstain on their manifesto and the photograph of John Looney—killed in Everett, Washington, in 1916—indicate the brutal results (pp. 31, 26). In Centralia, Washington, the I.W.W. tried to unionize timber workers, eventually leading to violence and six fatalities, including the lynching of Wesley Everest on November 11, 1919.

After threatening to strike, steelworkers back east, organized by the American Federation of Labor, walked off the job in September. That same month in Boston, when most of the police department failed to report for duty, hooliganism and rampant looting ensued until Massachusetts governor Calvin Coolidge called up the state militia.

African-American veterans faced hostility and did not receive a hero's welcome upon their return to the United States. Only 42,000 out of an estimated 200,000 soldiers saw combat, due to the racism of American military personnel who refused to fight alongside them. Many of those who fought did so under French command in integrated units. African-American journalist William Allison Sweeney argued that Woodrow Wilson's "War for Democracy," won in part by black soldiers, should

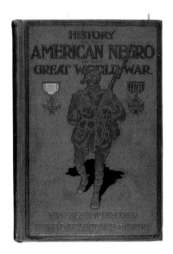

William Allison Sweeney, *History of the American Negro in the Great World War*, 1919, Cuneo-Henneberry, Chicago

28

(top left) "Enjoying a Bit of Cake Baked at the American Red
Cross Canteen, Is-sur-Tille, France"; (top right) "Corporal
Fred. McIntyre of 369th Infantry with Picture of the
Kaiser Which He Captured from a German Officer";
(bottom) "Going to Fight for Uncle Sam," in
Sweeney, *History of the American
Negro in the Great World War*

Chained to the Bars

WE
NEVER
FORGET

WE
NEVER
FORGET

Members of the I. W. W. have been subjected to this brutal treatment in the U. S. Penitentary at Leavenworth, Kas.

TO BE CHAINED TO A GIVEN SPOT IS PUNISHMENT.

To be Chained and Starved are Methods of the Spanish inquisition

Five weeks in this position during working hours on bread and water was the punishment inflicted upon two members of the Industrial Workers of the World.

Others suffered like treatment for shorter periods, afterward sentenced by the Deputy Warden L. J. Fletcher to permanent isolation. The Deputy Warden compelled two black men to severely beat with clubs the prisoners he had at his mercy.

... WE DEMAND RELIEF FOR THESE PRISONERS ...

The Chicago case has been appealed. The Sacramento case will be appealed. *Will you help to see that the new trials if granted are fair trials?*

Send all donations to
Gen'l Defense Com.,
1001 W. Madison St.
CHICAGO

Wm D Haywood.

Secretary General Defense Committee I. W. W.

ABOVE AND FACING
William D. Haywood, "Chained to the Bars" and "With Drops of Blood," 1919, fund-raising leaflets of the Industrial Workers of the World, Chicago

WITH DROPS OF BLOOD

THE HISTORY OF

THE INDUSTRIAL WORKERS OF THE WORLD HAS BEEN WRITTEN

Ever since the I. W. W. was organized in June, 1905, there has been an inquisitorial campaign against its life and growth, inaugurated by the Chambers of Commerce, Profiteers, large and small, and authorities of State and Nation in temporary power.

The Industrial Workers of the World is a Labor organization composed of sober, honest, industrious men and women. Its chief purposes are to abolish the system of wage slavery and to improve the conditions of those who toil.

This organization has been foully dealt with; drops of blood, bitter tears of anguish, frightful heart pains have marked its every step in its onward march of progress.

I. W. W. MEMBERS have been murdered.
I. W. W. MEMBERS have been imprisoned.
I. W. W. MEMBERS have been tarred and feathered.
I. W. W. MEMBERS have been deported
I. W. W. MEMBERS have been starved.
I. W. W. MEMBERS have been beaten.
I. W. W. MEMBERS have been denied the right of citizenship.
I. W. W. MEMBERS have been exiled.
I. W. W. MEMBERS have had their homes invaded.
I. W. W. MEMBERS have had their private property and papers seized.
I. W. W. MEMBERS have been denied the privilege of defense.
I. W. W. MEMBERS have been held in exorbitant bail.
I. W. W. MEMBERS have been subjected to involuntary servitude.
I. W. W. MEMBERS have been kidnapped.
I. W. W. MEMBERS have been subjected to cruel and unusual punishment.
I. W. W. MEMBERS have been "framed and unjustly accused.
I. W. W. MEMBERS have been excessively fined.
I. W. W. MEMBERS have died in jail waiting for trial.
I. W. W. MEMBERS have been driven insane through persecution.
I. W. W. MEMBERS have been denied the use of the mails.
I. W. W. MEMBERS have been denied the right to organize.
I. W. W. MEMBERS have been denied the right of free speech.
I. W. W. MEMBERS have been denied the right of free press.
I. W. W. MEMBERS have been denied the right of free assembly.
I. W. W. MEMBERS have been denied every privilege guaranteed by the Bill of Rights.
I. W. W. MEMBERS have been denied the inherent rights proclaimed by the Declaration of Independence—Life, Liberty, and the Pursuit of Happiness.
I. W. W. Halls, Offices and Headquarters have been raided.

I. W. W. property, books, pamphlets, stamps, literature, office fixtures have been unlawfully seized.

I. W. W. as an organization and its membership have been viciously maligned, vilified and persecuted.

December 21, 1919
—Emma Goldman
and 248 others are
deported under the
Immigration Act of
1918, which allows
for the expulsion of
"aliens" accused
of anarchism.

translate into improvements back home. "'Previous condition!' That the unpaid toil of thirty decades of African slavery in America is at last to be liquidated," he wrote.

Others were less sanguine. Writer, scholar, and public intellectual W. E. B. Du Bois knew that the fight had to continue, as he watched the situation deteriorate. The Red Summer of 1919—not to be confused with the anticommunist Red Scare—saw horrendous racial terrorism. This included lynchings, looting, and the destruction of African-American homes and businesses in rural Arkansas, Georgia, Texas, and Mississippi and in the cities of Chicago; Washington, D.C.; Charleston, South Carolina; Omaha, Nebraska; and San Francisco. The Equal Justice Initiative of Montgomery, Alabama, estimates that over two hundred African-American men, women, and children were murdered that summer. In response, membership in the National Association for the Advancement of Colored People (NAACP) increased exponentially.

Not every fight led to another. Suffragists took President Wilson to task for his "meaningless words on democracy," staging protests and exerting considerable pressure to pass a constitutional amendment to guarantee women the right to vote. Securing a two-thirds majority in the U.S. House of Representatives and Senate was a hard fight. A vote in February narrowly failed. *The Suffragist* magazine illustrated the struggle, from tussles with an indifferent Senate to successful passage in the House and Senate in May and then June, and, finally, to firecrackers going off to celebrate the first batch of state ratifications (pp. 42–43).

Charles H. Sykes, "At Last," in
The Suffragist, June 21, 1919,
National Woman's Party,
Washington, D.C.

LEFT
Technische Nothilfe sorgt für Wasser, Licht, und Wärme bei Stillegung lebenswichtiger Betriebe, 1919, lithograph, 28 ⅜ x 36 ¾ in., Ernst Neumann, Plakatkunstanstalt Dinse & Eckert, Germany

BELOW
Achtung! Stehenbleiben verboten! Auf Zusammenrottungen wird rücksichtslos geschossen (Warning! Stopping is prohibited! Crowds of rioters will be indiscriminately shot), 1919, lithograph, 27 ½ x 37 ¼ in., Germany

FACING
E. Weigand after K. Gellings, Le Havre, *Deutsches Hilfswerk für die Kriegs- und Zivilgefangenen* (German Welfare Organization for War and Civilian Prisoners), 1919, 54 x 35 ¾ in., J. Sauer Graphische Kunstanstalt GmBH, Berlin, Germany

Achtung!

Midnight blue on orange barks a threat. The poster at right was probably intended for a government building in Berlin during the German Revolution, when armed soldiers and paramilitary groups protected sensitive sites. For most of 1919, Germany was near civil war, with workers' council governments declared in Bremen, Munich, and Berlin. The kaiser's abdication, the collapse of the government, and the German surrender happened against a background of hunger and scarcity caused by the British naval blockade. Government and volunteer relief organizations issued pleas for help. Technische Nothilfe, which later allied with the Nazis, assisted with maintaining water, electricity, and heat during strikes and periods of disruption. Former soldiers and the Weimar government rallied to bring prisoners of war and civilian internees back home (p. 24). "They suffer for us!" the woeful poster at left declares. "To improve their lot is an obligation of honor."

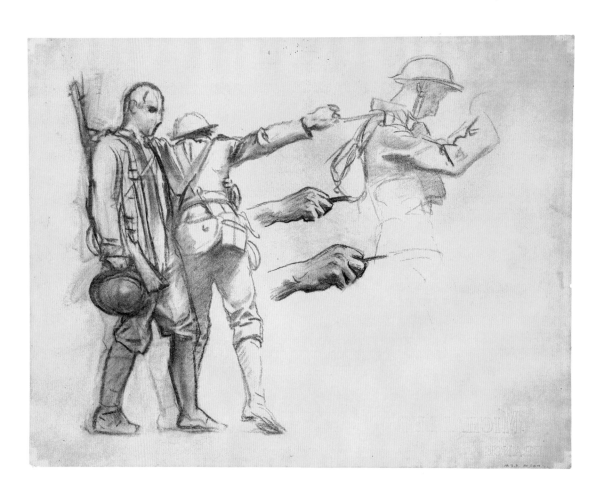

John Singer Sargent, *Study for Gassed*, ca. 1918–19, charcoal and stump on paper, 18 ¾ x 24 ⅜ in. Purchased with funds from the Virginia Steele Scott Foundation

This sketch, a preliminary drawing for a painting commissioned by the British War Memorials Committee, depicts a mustard gas attack, one of many such horrors Sargent encountered in a 1918 tour of the Western Front.

Percy John Smith, *Death Intoxicated*, 1919,
etching, 10 1/16 x 13 3/16 in., from the series The Dance
of Death, 1914–19. Gift of Russel I. Kully

Fatherless Children of France

World War I orphaned an estimated six million children, one million of whom were in France. In 1915, French officials and American patrons formed the Fatherless Children of France, a charity that sought donations from more than 180 U.S. chapters. The staff of Mount Wilson Observatory in Pasadena joined thousands of "godparents," or sponsors, in support of France's widows and their children. From 1917 to 1918, observatory staff "adopted" ten children, some of whom are shown here, and continued to support them through the mid-1920s. Letters in the Mount Wilson Collection at The Huntington indicate that astrophysicist Charles Edward St. John and librarian Elizabeth Connor organized the contributions ($36.50 was enough to cover one godchild for a year). Notes and photographs flowed between American sponsors and French families.

ABOVE
Paulette Marcelle Davy, 7, and Berthe Paule Davy, 5, 1919, gelatin silver print, 5 ½ x 3 ½ in.

BELOW
Renée and Pierre Durand, 1919, gelatin silver print, 3 ½ x 2 ⁵⁄₁₆ in.

Hélène and Félix Dumont, marked on the photograph with
a "+," were two of the French orphans supported
by Mount Wilson Observatory staff through
the Fatherless Children of
France charity.

JAILED FOR FREEDOM

Some Phases in the Front Line of a War for Democracy Not Quite Won

Burning President Wilson's Meaningless Words on Democracy

*National Woman's Party Members Demonstrating in Front of the
Lafayette Statue, Washington, D.C.*, September 16, 1918,
photograph reproduced in *Jailed for Freedom:
1919 Prison Special Edition of The Suffragist*

Votes for Women

On the first day of 1919, members of the National Woman's Party gathered outside the White House and burned President Woodrow Wilson's speeches in a marble urn. These suffragists considered Wilson's honeyed words about global democracy a bitter affront. In February, after the Nineteenth Amendment enfranchising women failed in the U.S. Senate once again, a small group of activists boarded the "Democracy Limited" train for a nationwide campaign. Their fifteen-city tour highlighted the beatings, imprisonments, and hunger strikes a courageous cohort had suffered to give women political voice. Decades of fighting finally paid off on June 4, 1919, when the Senate passed the amendment with fifty-six ayes over twenty-five nays. It was added to the Constitution on August 26, 1920, after its ratification by thirty-six states.

Trail Blazers

Journalist Delilah Leontium Beasley (1871–1934) spent "eight years and six months," by her own meticulous reckoning, in relentless pursuit of facts. After moving to Oakland from Cincinnati, Ohio, she traversed California "wherever a railroad or horse and buggy could go" to research the state's African-American pioneers. Her self-published book contains hundreds of biographical profiles and historical events compiled from archives, libraries, and first-person accounts. The author's collective portrait offered a sharp rebuke to the lynchings and race riots terrorizing black people during the bloody Red Summer of 1919. Beasley blazed a trail, too. Her volume still stands as a classic foundational text of history and civil rights.

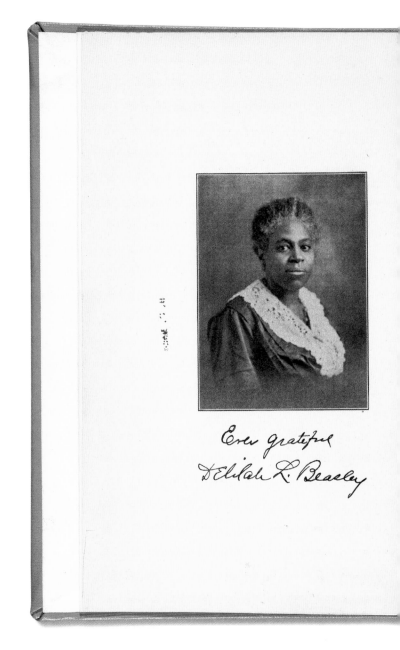

Ever grateful
Delilah L. Beasley

THE
NEGRO TRAIL BLAZERS
OF CALIFORNIA

Compilation of Records from the California Archives in the Bancroft
Library at the University of California, in Berkeley; and from the
Diaries, Old Papers and Conversations of Old Pioneers in
the State of California. It is a True Record of
Facts, as They Pertain to the History of
the Pioneer and Present Day
Negroes of California

BY
DELILAH L. BEASLEY

Los Angeles, California
1919

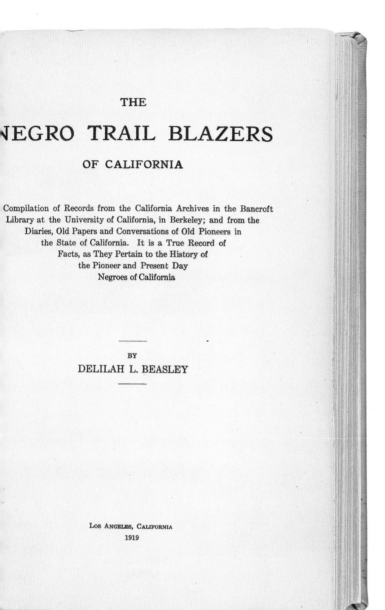

HON. JOHN WESLEY COLEMAN
The Old Reliable Employment Agent of Los Angeles.

MME. ELLA BRADLEY-HUGHLEY (deceased)
Vocal Instructor, Lyric Soprano.

ABOVE
"Hon. John Wesley Coleman,
The Old Reliable Employment
Agent of Los Angeles"

BELOW
"Mme Ella Bradley-Hughley
(deceased), Vocal Instructor,
Lyric Soprano"

FACING
"Delilah L. Beasley," in Delilah L.
Beasley, *The Negro Trail Blazers
of California*, 1919

Enemy Aliens

President Woodrow Wilson ordered all non-naturalized German men aged fourteen and older to register as enemies of the United States on November 16, 1917. The arrest records of the U.S. Marshal's office in Los Angeles indicate the age, physical attributes, and employment of numerous "alien enemies," as they were called. These immigrants—mostly single and aged twenty-five to thirty-five—were jailed because their nationality posed "a danger to the public peace and safety of the United States." The proclamation became void shortly after the armistice in November 1918. Even so, these Los Angeles waiters, fruit dealers, day laborers, and clerks had to file for parole. Most were not released from federal surveillance until the spring of 1919.

ABOVE
(from top) *Kurt Paul Kunsman,
William Engelbrecht*

LEFT
(clockwise from top left) *Gustav
Hartwig, Henry Rattau, Rudolf Mothes,
Phillip Sojat*, all in Office of U.S.
Marshal, Register of Prisoners
in County Jails, 1918–22, gelatin
silver prints

FOLLOWING SPREADS
(page 48) "Gas Mask of Flannelette
Type for Horse"; (page 49) "The
Akron Tissot Mask, an Improvement
Over the Mask That Was in General
Use among Our Troops," in Benedict
Crowell, *America's Munitions 1917–1918,*
1919, Government Printing Office,
Washington, D.C.; (pages 50–51)
C. C. Pierce, *English Trench near
Ypres, A.E.F. in France,* 1919, gelatin
silver print, 5 x 6 ⅞ in.; (pages 52–53)
"The End of the War," in *America's
Munitions 1917–1918*

Bernard L. Boldt,
724 Wall St.,
11-25) 441 Stanford Ave
647 San Pedro St.
Richter Mch. Co
7th street

Reports every week

	1 - 8	8 - 15	15 - 22	22 - 31
Sept.	Reported ___ To	Reported ___ To	Reported ___ To	Reported ___ To
Oct.	Reported 7 To Menick	Reported 14 To Menick	Reported 21 To Menick	Reported 28 To Menick
Nov.	Reported 4 To Kelty	Reported 12 To Menick	Reported 18 To Menick	Reported 25 To Menick
Dec.	Reported 2 To Menick	Reported 9 To Menick	Reported 16 To Menick	Reported 23 To Menick
Jan. 1919	Reported 6 To Menick	Reported 13 To Sittel	Reported 20 To Kelty	Reported 27 To Menick
Feb.	Reported 3 To Menick	Reported 10 To Menick	Reported 17 To Menick	Reported 24 To Kelty
March	Reported 3 To Sittel	Reported 10 To Cavanaugh	Reported 17 To Menick	Reported 24-31 To Menick - M.
April	Reported 7 To Menick	Reported 14 To Menick	Reported ___ To Cancelld	Reported ___ To April 17, 1919
May	Reported ___ To	Reported ___ To	Reported ___ To	Reported ___ To
June	Reported ___ To	Reported ___ To	Reported ___ To	Reported ___ To
July	Reported ___ To	Reported ___ To	Reported ___ n To	Reported ___ To

Office of U.S. Marshal, Register of Prisoners
in County Jails, Federal Warrant No. 84,
Bernard Ludwig Boldt, Parole
Record, 1918–19

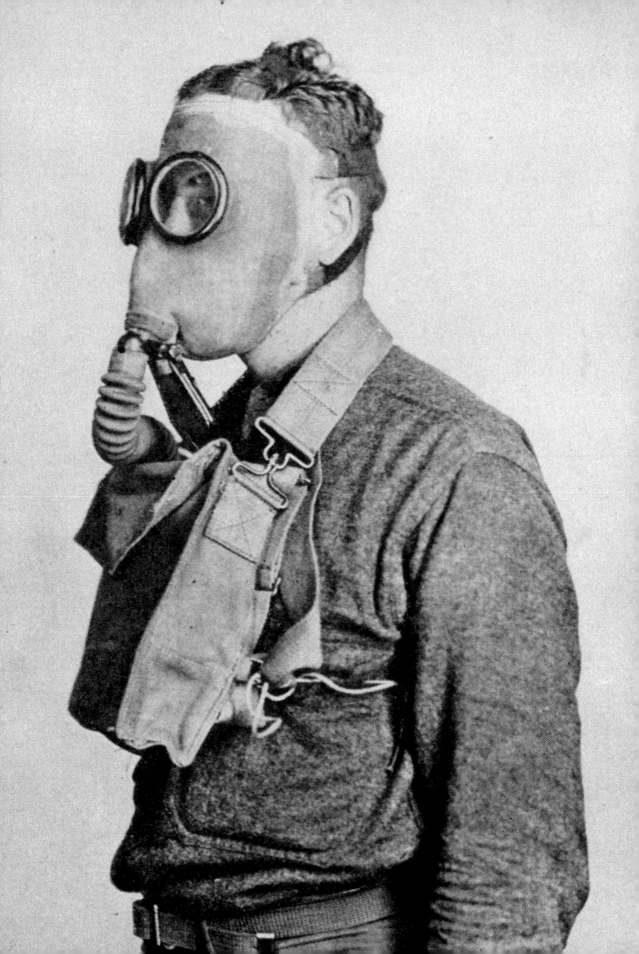

"THE END OF THE WAR."

A GRAPHIC RECORD.

Nov. 11, 1918.
11 A. M.

One minute before
the hour.
All guns firing.

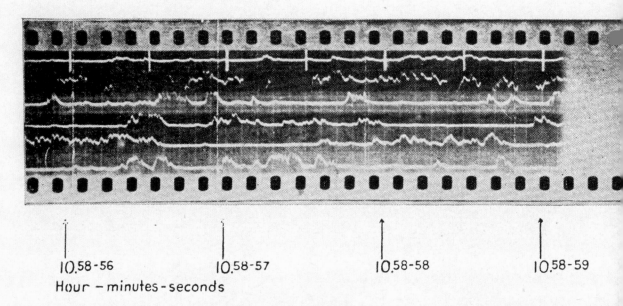

10.58-56   10.58-57   10.58-58   10.58-59

Hour – minutes - seconds

This is the last record by sound ranging of artillery activity on the America
as it issued from an American sound-ranging apparatus when the hou
cease firing, and the great war came to an end. Six seconds of sound r
artillery activity; the lack of irregularities on the right indicates almos
to the exuberance of a doughboy firing his pistol twice close to one of t
minutes on either side of the exact armistice hour have been cut from t
ing the positions and calibers of enemy guns. A description of these w
III, chapter 4

One minute after
the hour.
All guns silent.

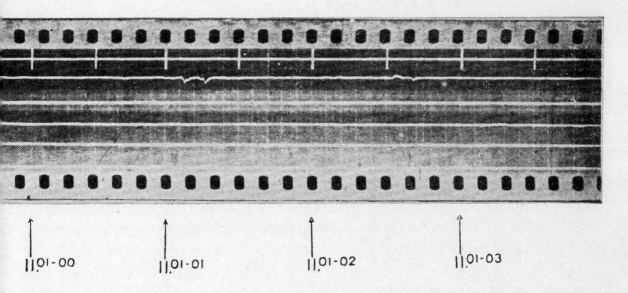

↑   ↑   ↑   ↑
11.01-00   11.01-01   11.01-02   11.01-03

ear the River Moselle. It is the reproduction of a piece of recording tape
clock on the morning of November 11, 1918, brought the general order to
are shown. The broken character of the records on the left indicates great
e cessation of firing, the two breaks in the second line probably being due
ng microphones on the front in celebration of the dawn of peace. The two
emphasize the contrast. Sound ranging was an important means of locat-
devices, which were a secret with America and the Allies, is given in Book

BELOW
Keystone View Co., *Happy Reunion for Home-
Coming Soldier Fathers*, ca. 1919, from
World War through the Stereoscope, gelatin
silver print, 3 ½ x 7 in.

FACING
Keystone View Co., *Some of Our Two Million Fighters
Ready for Home, Brest, France*, ca. 1919,
from World War through the Stereoscope, gelatin
silver print, 3 ½ x 7 in.

Henry Huntington

Henry Huntington hoped, like many Americans, that 1919 would see a return to better days. The United States had helped defeat Germany and its allies, putting punitive sanctions into place. Even so, inflation, labor issues, and racial violence threatened postwar calm. Huntington harbored doubts about what was to come.

An acquaintance tried to diagnose Huntington's frame of mind. "I cannot but think that the real cause of your distemper . . . is rooted in your THOUGHTS," the man wrote. Musing on present conditions had stirred up the sixty-nine-year-old Huntington. "These are not ordinary times," his correspondent insisted. "Everything in the world is in a state of flux. . . . What will eventually come out of it all, no man on earth can even begin to say."

Perhaps Huntington longed to turn back the clock to before the Great War. In Paris, on July 16, 1913, he had married Belle, his uncle's widow, after actively courting her for seven years. "I am just beginning to live," he wrote his sister while honeymooning in France. "Life seems so very very sweet."

Huntington promptly leased Château Beauregard to please his Francophile bride. The 400-acre estate, located not far from Versailles, once belonged to Napoléon III. Huntington rented it for $35,000 a year.

While the newlywed couple motored around Europe in the summer of 1914, Germany declared war on France. The Huntingtons reluctantly decamped and sailed for home.

The Great War proved lucrative to the capitalist and serial entrepreneur. The Newport News Shipbuilding and Dry Dock Company, which he and Arabella had inherited from Collis, ramped up production of battleships to fulfill government contracts.

At war's end, millions came streaming back from the trenches and battlefields, forever changed by the horrors they had seen. Volunteers and soldiers yearned for normalcy. They wanted hope.

Huntington pushed his melancholy aside. He believed that the time to announce his library and art gallery, a noble "temple to learning," was finally right.

<u>Arabella Huntington</u>

Belle and Edward supported the war effort to some
extent. Edward granted permission for refugees
to camp at Château Beauregard, in the stables and
fields. Together they gave $120,000 to the Red
Cross. They donated an ambulance to the American
Committee for Devastated France. The little Ford,
sporting an insignia of a cowboy lassoing a fleeing
Wilhelm II, had "Henry E. Huntington, Los Angeles"
painted on its sides. It transported the dead and
wounded for three long years.

When the Great War ended, Arabella Huntington
welcomed soldiers and nurses home with open arms.
She set down a policy for her New York staff: any
returning man or woman who came to her Fifth Avenue
palace would be given coffee, money, and a meal.
Belle insisted that each person be ushered into the
opulent dining room and fed.

In August 1919, the couple traveled to Southern
California for round after round of celebratory
events marking the return of the Pacific Fleet.
At a quieter moment, they signed a legal document
making their private estate a public institution
dedicated to learning and the arts.

1919 ——————— Return

Goodbye Czar, King, and Kaiser,
Now we trust you all are wiser.
Goodbye cooties, rats, and stenches,
no more muddy, bloody, trenches.
Goodbye gas bombs torture filling,
no more zeppelins baby killing.

—Lou Spero, lyrics to
"Good-bye, Shot and Shell!," 1919

In Flanders fields the poppies blow
Between the crosses, row on row,
That mark our place; and in the sky
The larks still bravely singing fly,
Scarce heard amidst the guns below.

—John McCrae,
"In Flanders Fields," 1915

When, when, and whenever death
closes our eyelids,
Moving naked over Acheron
    Upon the one raft, victor and
conquered together,
Marius and Jugurtha together,
        one tangle of shadows.

—Ezra Pound,
Homage to Sextus Propertius, 1919

THE ARCH OF VICTORY AND ADJACENT PYLONS AT MADISON SQUARE, ADORNED WITH

EAPONS AND NAMES OF BATTLES IN WHICH THE TROOPS PARTICIPATED, MAR. 25, 1919.

Cyrus Le Roy Baldridge, *Study of a Soldier*, 1919, gouache
and graphite on paper, 19 x 13 3/4 in. Purchased with
funds from the Virginia Steele Scott Foundation

The global war machine could not be stopped quickly once the armistice was signed on November 11, 1918. Back in the United States, despite demobilization, wartime production contracts were extended through January and some into summer to avoid a flood of unemployment as four million veterans sought jobs. Ports of arrival on France's Atlantic coast that had dealt with incoming soldiers now reversed the process; doughboys received discharge papers, new clothes, and a thorough delousing before boarding passenger ships bound for America. Cooties, as lice were called, spread typhus, an acute and sometimes fatal bacterial infection. By the end of the year, most of the two million Americans in Europe had recrossed the Atlantic, to be greeted by rapturous victory parades and receptions (pp. 62–63).

Some remained overseas. Cyrus Le Roy Baldridge, an illustrator for the Army newspaper *Stars and Stripes*, sketched an American military policeman in Koblenz, a German town on the Rhine that was occupied by U.S. troops. Many never came home, buried in graveyards and ossuaries across France and Belgium. The popular poem "In Flanders Fields," with its image of poppies fluttering on soldiers' graves and desolate trenches, turned the red flower into a symbol of sacrifice (p. 67).

Those who survived tried to understand the war and its repercussions. Yearbook-type publications commemorated the experiences of soldiers, as in *History of the 42d: The Rainbow Division* and *24 Days on a Troop Ship*. Other books helped with reintegration. *Where Do We Go from Here? This Is the Real Dope* gave soon-to-be-discharged soldiers instructions on receiving final pay, obtaining artificial limbs, and signing up for vocational training (p. 82). Trench humor, like *Fragments from France* or songs about cooties, feel profoundly off-key. How could such suffering be a laughing matter? As Paul Fussell's classic study *The Great War and Modern Memory* cautions, humor softened overwhelming tragedy and the possibility—even near certainty—of dying.

January 6, 1919—
Former President Theodore Roosevelt dies in his sleep.

February 17, 1919—
The African-American 369th Infantry, known as the "Harlem Hellfighters," return from war after spending more time in combat than any other American unit.

April 1919—
A Huntington librarian, Chester M. Cate, rejoins the staff after serving with the U.S. Army Hospital Corps.

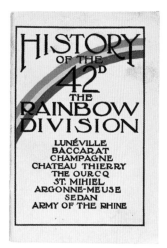

ABOVE

(left) Walter B. Wolf, *History of the 42d: The Rainbow Division*, 1919, Rand, McNally, New York; (middle) Bruce Bairnsfather, *Fragments from France*, 1917–19, G. P. Putnam's Sons, New York; (right) J. Ralph Pickell, *Twenty-Four Days on a Troopship*, 1919, Rosenbaum Review, Chicago

October 1–9, 1919—Eight players for the Chicago White Sox intentionally lose the World Series against the Cincinnati Reds in a match-fixing scheme known as the "Black Sox Scandal."

Elation, survivor's guilt, and simple anxiety about finding a job colored each soldier's return. In 1919, Sigmund Freud, that controversial soothsayer of the mind, identified a mental state in which life and death, comfort and unease mingle. He said that this state "recalls the sense of helplessness sometimes experienced in dreams," caused by the "recurrence of the same situation," which was once familiar but now made strange. Freud's concept of the *uncanny*, as he called it, surely applied to the world-weary American soldiers who returned to their largely unchanged hometowns and families who knew nothing of trench warfare or poison gas.

Where to turn when the present felt like a bad dream? Popular song lyrics gave one avenue of escape (pp. 68–69). *Let the Rest of the World Go By* pines for the comforts of a new, different home, a place of safety and contentment: "We'll find perfect peace, Where joys never cease." *I'm Forever Blowing Bubbles* finds solace in the ephemeral: "I'm dreaming dreams, I'm scheming schemes, I'm building castles high; they're born anew, their days are few, just like a sweet butterfly."

A 1919 edition of Jules Verne's novel *The Mysterious Island* (1874) begins with N. C. Wyeth's cover illustration

66

Keep the Faith, with excerpt from "In Flanders Fields"
by John McCrae, ca. 1919, Liberty Loan Committee,
Second Federal Reserve District, New York

Jaan Kenbrovin (James Kendis, James Brockman,
and Nat Vincent) and John William Kellette,
I'm Forever Blowing Bubbles, 1919, Jerome H.
Remick & Co., New York and Detroit

68

Return

of a balloon crashing into a storm-tossed Pacific (p. 85). Flipping the book open to the endsheets shows the castaways safely landed on a beach—except the story is not so simple. While the adults trudge forward, the boy glances back, as if he senses danger lurking on the island. Like postwar Europe, this motley crew is not yet in the clear, as unseen forces hover in the margins.

Childhood and fantasy are the ultimate places of safety, and 1919 saw the publication of a number of beautiful children's books. An updated edition of Nathaniel Hawthorne's *Tanglewood Tales* reworked timeless Greek myths for children. Edmund Dulac's illustrations, inspired by Minoan wall paintings, conjure a faraway world in which the gods mete out brutal justice to mortals who violate the divine order (p. 84). This vision perhaps reflected a longing for blunt and effective fixes to the postwar moment's intractable problems. There were no gods to settle matters for humankind—only the politicians in Versailles and Washington.

Canonical tradition and myth continued to nourish artists, despite the revolution of modernist art in the years before the war. The choreographer Ruth St. Denis borrowed poses and costumes from ancient Egyptian and Indian cultures (pp. 88–89). John Singer Sargent took up the age-old strategy of allegory when he depicted the enigmatic sphinx and malevolent chimaera in a public mural that referred to the ancient Egyptian and Greek collections at the Museum of Fine Arts, Boston (pp. 90–91).

Returning to the past also provided a wellspring for the American-born British poet and playwright T. S. Eliot. In "Tradition and the Individual Talent," he asserted that, to speak broadly and fully, a poet needed to converse with literary history. Great writers work inside and not against tradition. In 1919, Ezra Pound, a friend of Eliot's, loosely translated the elegies of the ancient Roman poet Sextus Propertius. The Latin author's light tone and sophisticated irony put the endless wars and corrupt

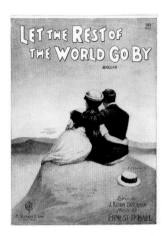

J. Keirn Brennan and Ernest R. Ball, *Let the Rest of the World Go By*, 1919, M. Witmark & Sons, New York

October 2, 1919— President Woodrow Wilson suffers a stroke; the seriousness of his condition is hidden from the public and Congress.

November 11, 1919— U.S. citizens commemorate the first Armistice Day, later celebrated as Veterans Day.

politics of Rome at arm's length, presenting a parallel to the recently concluded Great War and ensuing chaos. In Pound's poem, Marius, a Roman consul, and Jugurtha, a vanquished foe of Rome, float in the same boat on Acheron, a river of the underworld. Like European nations still stuck together after four years of war, these erstwhile adversaries are now "one tangle of shadows," uncomfortably knotted together for eternity.

71

Return

Victory Loans

The U.S. Treasury's Liberty Loan program spurred citizens to buy war bonds through four fundraising campaigns. A fifth subscription—the Victory Loan—was organized after the cease-fire in November 1918. Posters like *To the Folks Back Home* (p. 71) and *Americans All!* plastered public spaces, urging the purchase of bonds from $5 to $100,000. Others, like *The Spirit of America*, asked for different kinds of aid—in this case, urging women to join the Red Cross. Howard Chandler Christy (1873–1952), the leading illustrator behind the success of these posters, was known for his "Christy Girls." He drew sailor-suited cheerleaders, nurses, angels, and allegorical figures such as Liberty and Justice. The public responded to Christy's subtly erotic beauties: all five loan campaigns were oversubscribed, and $17 billion was raised. Yet his fantasy girls also obscured the hard work and gritty realities of thousands of flesh-and-blood women who served the war effort in various capacities.

RIGHT
Howard Chandler Christy, *Americans All!*, 1919, lithograph, 40 x 26 ⅞ in., Forbes Lithograph Manufacturing, Boston

FACING
Howard Chandler Christy, *The Spirit of America—Join*, 1919, lithograph, 30 x 20 in., Forbes Lithograph Manufacturing for the American Red Cross, Boston

FOLLOWING SPREAD
"Negro Nurses Carrying Banner of Famous Negro Regiment Marching Down Fifth Avenue New York," in Sweeney, *History of the American Negro in the Great World War*

The Great War, Month by Month

An unpublished, 800-page illustrated typescript was Roland S. Gielow's idiosyncratic attempt to make meaning out of the chaos of global conflict. During the war, Gielow (1883–1940), in his mid-thirties, was running a blueprint office. Like many Americans, he avidly followed the battle from home through periodicals, newsreels, and "letters from officers 'over there.'" These sources became the basis for a detailed account of all fifty-one months of the war. The draftsman's record is systematic,

archival, encyclopedic, even obsessive, with an assortment of meticulous lists, charts, and hand-drawn maps. It reveals his interest in aesthetics alongside tactics and statistics. He renders maps, badges, and battleships in intricate, colorful detail—employing a variety of painterly styles and flourishes. An engineer for the city of Long Beach, Gielow later won a contest to design the municipal seal; it is still in use today.

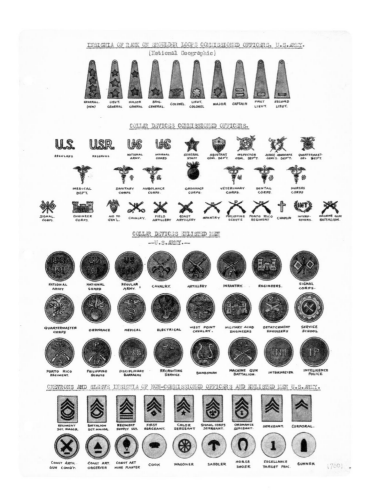

LEFT, FACING, AND FOLLOWING SPREAD
Pages from Roland S. Gielow, "Historic Events of the World War 1914–1918," loose-leaf typescript, 1919

Return

In Reims, Chalons, and other citires, miles behind the trenches, the school children were obliged to carry gas-masks in their pockets or satchels. The writer says:

"This simple fact shows the danger of gas-shells to a vast area of civilian population miles and miles behind the front, from the Atlantic to Belfort. How many miles deep is this danger-zone to farmers, villagers, townsmen, and school babies. Big long distance guns can throw these poison-shells 8 miles, 12 miles, without prohibitive expense - and they do it!"   • • • • • • • •

JUL 15.   Allies Occupy Murman Coast. Dispatches of July 15 confirmed earlier reports that British and American naval forces in the Arctic had landed troops and occupied the Murman coast and parts of the Murman railroad. This was done with the approval of the local population, whose interests are with the Allies, and with the object of preventing supplies in Arctic ports from falling into hostile hands, guarding the only western communications between Russia and the Allies, and shutting Germany off from a possible submarine base in the Arctic. Thus at the same time a route is kept open for further aid to Russia.

American and British troops have occupied the whole of the Murman coast, in Northern Russia, says a despatch from Moscow to the Central News Agency by way of Amsterdam.

After capturing Kem, a railroad station on the White Sea cost, the dispatch adds, the American and British forces advanced toward Toroki, the Russian Bolshevist authorities having withdrawn to Nirok.

The commanders of the Entente allied forces have issued an appeal to the population on the Murman coast requesting help against Germany and Finland. It is declared that the Murman coast is Russian territory under the protection of the Entente Powers.

M. Tschitcherin, the Russian Foreign Minister, has addressed a note to Great Britain demanding that the British detachments now on the Murman coast be re-embarked without delay.

THE MURMAN COAST AND RAILWAY. Having just arrived from the Murman district, in the north of Russia, V. Goriachkovsky, chief engineer of the Murman railroad system, was able yesterday to confirm the reports that the entire Murman population is eagerly appealing for Allied intervention. "I am not in the least surprised that the population of Murman has proclaimed openly for the Allies," he declared. "The people there are hostile to Bolshevism, and, being remotely located from the Soviet machine in Moscow, have not yet been terrorized by Red Guards. Spending nearly two years among them, I could not help being impressed with their outspoken loyalty to the cause of the Allies.

"This devotion has been developed, not only by reason of their patriotic faith in the cause of the Allies, but also by reason of the fact that since the revolution and even before the Murman population has received almost all of its food and supplies from America and the other Allies. So far as the Soviet Government in Moscow is concerned, the Murman district is left to starve, and would starve if it were not for the food that is coming through the ice-free port of Mourmansk from the Allies.

"This is true to such an extent that the people in the Murman region feel much closer to New York than they do to Moscow, and are accustomed to look to the Allies for friendship and help rather than to the government which now assumes to rule in Russia.

(408)

TABULATION OF UNITS ASSIGNED TO DIVISIONS

The following table, issued by the Statistics Branch of the War Department, shows the units included in each division.

DIVISIONS	INFANTRY BRIGADES		INFANTRY REGIMENTS				MACHINE-GUN BATTALIONS			ARTILLERY BRIGADES	ARTILLERY REGIMENTS			TRENCH MORTAR BATTERY AND TRAINS	ENGINEER REG. AND TRAINS	FIELD SIGNAL BATTALION	AMBULANCE COMPANIES & FIELD HOSPITALS				DIVISIONS
1	1	2	16	18	26	28	1	2	3	1	5	6	7	1	1	2	3	4	12	13	1
2	3	4	9	23	(5)	(6)	4	5	6	2	15	17	12	2	2	1	1	15	16	23	2
3	5	6	4	7	30	38	7	8	9	3	10	76	18	3	6	5	5	7	26	27	3
4	7	8	39	47	58	59	10	11	12	4	16	77	13	4	4	8	19	21	28	33	4
5	9	10	60	61	6	11	13	14	15	5	19	20	21	5	7	9	17	25	29	30	5
6	11	12	51	52	53	54	16	17	18	6	3	78	11	6	318	6	20	37	38	40	6
7	13	14	55	56	34	64	19	20	21	7	79	80	8	7	5	10	22	34	35	36	7
8	15	16	12	62	8	13	22	23	24	8	2	81	83	8	319	320	11	31	32	43	8
9	17	18	45	46	67	68	25	26	27	9	25	26	27	9	209	209	233	234	235	236	9
10	19	20	20	41	69	70	28	29	30	10	28	29	30	10	210	210	237	238	239	240	10
11	21	22	17	63	71	72	31	32	33	11	31	32	33	11	211	211	241	242	243	244	11
12	23	24	36	42	73	74	34	35	36	12	34	35	36	12	212	212	245	246	247	248	12
13	25	26	1	44	75	76	37	38	39	13	37	38	39	13	213	213	249	250	251	252	13
14	27	28	10	40	77	78	40	41	42	14	40	41	42	14	214	214	253	254	255	256	14
15	29	30	43	79	57	80	43	44	45	15	43	44	45	15	215	215	257	258	259	260	15
16	31	32	21	81	32	82	46	47	48	16	46	47	48	16	216	216	261	262	263	264	16
17	33	34	5	83	29	84	49	50	51	17	49	50	51	17	217	217	265	266	267	268	17
18	35	36	19	85	35	86	52	53	54	18	52	53	54	18	218	218	269	270	271	272	18
19	37	38	14	87	2	88	55	56	57	19	55	56	57	19	219	219	273	274	275	276	19
20	39	40	48	89	50	90	58	59	60	20	58	59	60	20	220	220	277	278	279	280	20
26	51	52	101	102	103	104	101	102	103	51	101	102	103	101	101	101	101	102	103	104	26
27	53	54	105	106	107	108	104	105	106	52	104	105	106	102	102	102	105	106	107	108	27
28	55	56	109	110	111	112	107	108	109	53	107	108	109	103	103	103	109	110	111	112	28
29	57	58	113	114	115	116	110	111	112	54	110	111	112	104	104	104	113	114	115	116	29
30	59	60	117	118	119	120	113	114	115	55	113	114	115	105	105	105	117	118	119	120	30
31	61	62	121	122	123	124	116	117	118	56	116	117	118	106	106	106	121	122	123	124	31
32	63	64	125	126	127	128	119	120	121	57	119	120	121	107	107	107	125	126	127	128	32
33	65	66	129	130	131	132	122	123	124	58	122	123	124	108	108	108	129	130	131	132	33
34	67	68	133	134	135	136	125	126	127	59	125	126	127	109	109	109	133	134	135	136	34
35	69	70	137	138	139	140	128	129	130	50	128	129	130	110	110	110	137	138	139	140	35
36	71	72	141	142	143	144	131	132	133	61	131	132	133	111	111	111	141	142	143	144	36
37	73	74	145	146	147	148	134	135	136	62	134	135	136	112	112	112	145	146	147	148	37
38	75	76	149	150	151	152	137	138	139	63	137	138	139	113	113	113	149	150	151	152	38
39	77	78	153	154	155	156	140	141	142	64	140	141	142	114	114	114	153	154	155	156	39
40	79	80	157	158	159	160	143	144	145	65	143	144	145	115	115	115	157	158	159	160	40
41	81	82	161	162	163	164	146	147	148	66	146	147	148	116	116	116	161	162	163	164	41
42	83	84	165	166	167	168	149	150	151	67	149	150	151	117	117	117	165	166	167	168	42

(Continued next page)

(764)

78

LIBERTY LOAN BUTTONS.

SERVICE FLAGS.

KILLED IN ARMY.   IN ARMY.   KILLED IN NAVY.   IN NAVY.

THE LIBERTY LOANS BY FEDERAL RESERVE DISTRICTS.

City Districts –	First Loan. (June 1917) 3½ percent	Second Loan. October 1917 4 per cent.	Third Loan. (1918) 4¼ per cent.	Fourth Loan. (1918) 4¼ per cent.
BOSTON	$ 333,447,600	$ 476,950,050	$ 354,537,250	$ 632,221,850
NEW YORK	1,186,788,400	1,550,453,450	1,115,243,650	2,004,778,000
PHILADELPHIA	232,309,250	380,350,250	361,963,500	598,763,650
CLEVELAND	286,148,700	486,106,800	405,051,150	702,059,800
RICHMOND	109,737,100	201,212,500	186,259,050	352,688,200
ATLANTA	57,878,550	90,695,750	137,649,450	213,885,200
CHICAGO	357,195,950	585,853,350	608,878,600	969,209,000
ST. LOUIS	86,134,700	184,280,750	199,835,900	296,388,550
MINNEAPOLIS	70,255,500	140,932,650	180,892,100	241,028,300
KANSAS CITY	91,758,850	150,125,750	204,092,800	294,646,450
DALLAS	48,948,350	77,899,850	116,220,650	145,944,450
SAN FRANCISCO	175,623,900	292,671,150	287,975,000	459,000,000
TOTAL SUBSCRIPTIONS	3,035,226,850	4,617,532,300	4,176,516,850	6,989,047,000
TOTAL QUOTAS	2,000,000,000	3,000,000,000	3,000,000,000	6,000,000,000
TOTAL ALLOTMENTS	3,035,226,850	3,808,766,150	4,176,516,850	6,989,047,000
TOTAL NO. OF SUBSCRIBERS	4,500,000	10,020,000	17,000,000	21,000,000

Apl. 20, 1919 – FIFTH LIBERTY LOAN (victory loan) – The United States Government issued 4¾% Bonds for 4,500,000,000.00. The amount subscribed was $5,249,908,300.00.

(805)

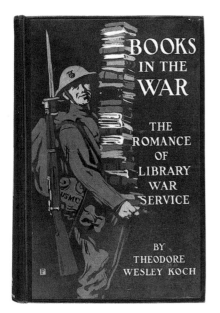

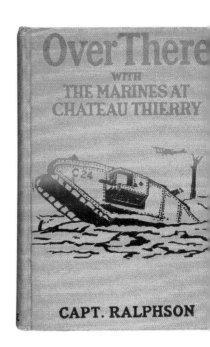

SEA-HOUNDS

LIEUT. LEWIS R. FREEMAN

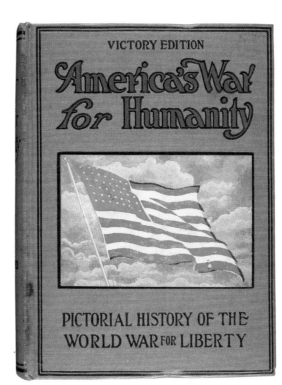

VICTORY EDITION

America's War
for Humanity

PICTORIAL HISTORY OF THE
WORLD WAR FOR LIBERTY

WHERE
DO
WE GO
FROM
HERE

This is the re

William
Late Major

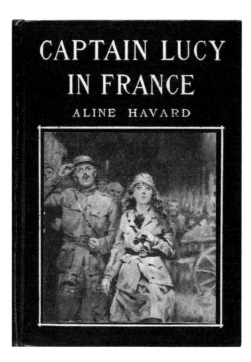

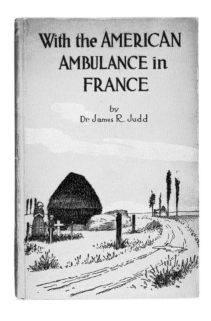

Return

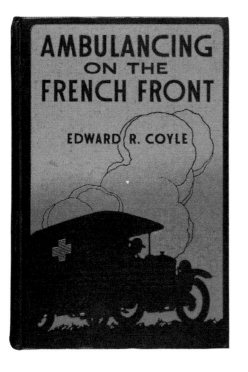

Edmund Dulac, cover and frontispiece
of Tiphys piloting the *Argo*, in
Nathaniel Hawthorne, *Tanglewood
Tales*, ca. 1919, Hodder and Stoughton,
London

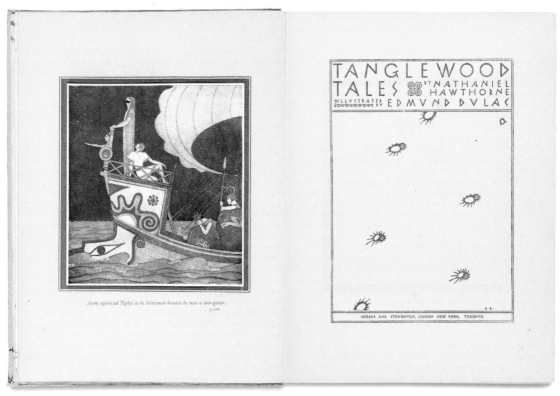

N. C. Wyeth, cover and endpapers,
in Jules Verne, *The Mysterious Island*,
1919, Scribner's Sons, New York

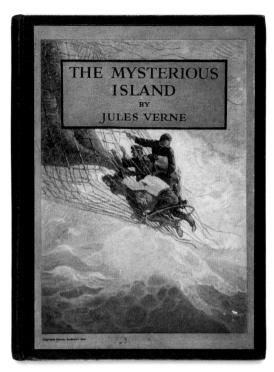

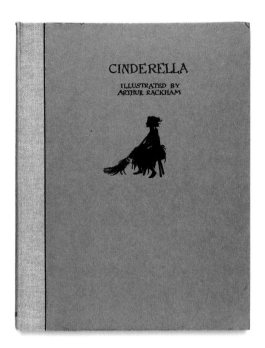

LEFT AND FACING
Arthur Rackham, illustrations,
in C. S. Evans, *Cinderella*, 1919,
W. Heinemann, London

Storybook Cinderella

Born into a working-class London family, Arthur Rackham (1867–1939) identified as a Cockney. Though he attended the Lambeth School of Art, his limited means forced him to work as an insurance clerk while slowly building a profile contributing illustrations to periodicals. By the time *Cinderella* was published in 1919, Rackham commanded high fees and had an international following, especially in the United States. The illustrations reproduced at the top of the facing page display Rackham's two signature styles. The first is organic, with the interwoven forms of mice, lizards, and patterns along a dark border that surrounds Cinderella in her rags, looking out a window. His second style features sharply edged, animated silhouettes. Many critics have noted the resemblance between Rackham's silhouettes and the work of contemporary African-American artist Kara Walker (b. 1969), whose powerful art addresses the history of enslavement and violence in the United States.

86

Return

BELOW
Robert Henri, "The Peacock Dance,"
in Ted Shawn, *Ruth St. Denis: Pioneer
and Prophet*, vol. 2, 1920, John Henry
Nash, San Francisco

FACING
Edward Weston, *Ruth St. Denis*, 1919,
palladium print, 8 ⅞ x 7 ⅜ in.

Modern Dancer

Ruth St. Denis (1879–1968) looked back to India, Egypt, Japan, and ancient Greece to inspire the theatrical, free-flowing performances that made her a progenitor of modern dance. With her partner and husband, Ted Shawn (1891–1972), she founded the Denishawn School in Los Angeles in 1915. While Shawn spent the war years in France with the 158th Ambulance Company, St. Denis sold over $100,000 worth of Liberty bonds in the lobby of the Alexandria Hotel in downtown Los Angeles. She continued to teach and dance, and she posed for photographer Edward Weston (1886–1958), another rising star. The photographer, still in the dreamy, soft-focus phase of his early career, arranged St. Denis's gauzy "teaching costume" to mirror the canvas tent of the outdoor studio arcing above. The dancer gazes directly at the camera with the self-assurance of an iconoclastic pioneer.

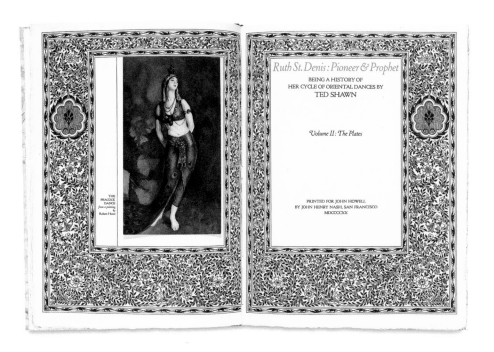

THE PEACOCK DANCE
from a painting by
Robert Henri

Ruth St. Denis: Pioneer & Prophet
BEING A HISTORY OF
HER CYCLE OF ORIENTAL DANCES BY
TED SHAWN

Volume II: The Plates

PRINTED FOR JOHN HOWELL
BY JOHN HENRY NASH, SAN FRANCISCO
MDCCCCXX

Ancient Modern

This circular oil study is for one of eight paintings
made by John Singer Sargent (1856–1925) for the
rotunda at the Museum of Fine Arts, Boston. Sargent
frequently mixed mythologies in his later work,
as seen in this canvas. The choice of the sphinx and
chimaera reflects his travels in Egypt and Greece
in 1890. The imaginary creatures also visually link
the museum to two ancient civilizations. In myths,
the chimaera is a winged monster and a portent of
danger. Sargent turns the fearsome beast into an
angelic figure that gracefully conforms to the painting's circular format and whose youthful, nude
body references Greco-Roman sculpture. The sphinx
reflects the West's interest in ancient Egypt, kindled
by the emerging disciplines of archaeology and art
history. Though awarded the museum commission
in 1916, Sargent likely made this particular study in
1919, after finishing work as an official war artist
for Great Britain. The entire project—which included
sculptural reliefs and architectural elements also
designed by the painter—was unveiled in 1921 to
wide acclaim.

FACING
John Singer Sargent, *Sphinx and
Chimaera*, 1916–21, oil on canvas, diam.
35 ½ in. Purchased with funds from
the Virginia Steele Scott Foundation
and Mr. and Mrs. Harry Spiro

FOLLOWING SPREADS
(pages 92–93) "Soldiers Who Had
Been in Training at Camp Dix, N.J.,
Receiving Their Honorable Discharge
Papers," in *The War of the Nations*;
(pages 94–95) "New York's Tribute to
Home-Coming Soldiers: Arch
of Jewels at Sixtieth Street and Fifth
Avenue," in *The War of the Nations*

Return

91

Arabella Huntington

The first two decades of Arabella's life are *terra incognita*, hazy at best. She seems to have sailed off the map of her history and never looked back.

An intelligent, striking young woman with a magnetic personality and plenty of Southern charm, Belle maneuvered her way out of an unsavory childhood with dashing gambler Johnny Worsham by her side.

In 1870, Belle had a baby, her coddled only child. She changed his name to Archer M. Worsham after Johnny left for good. Belle set a direct course for Collis P. Huntington, one of America's wealthiest men.

"I am ashamed to ask you," she penned Collis in 1871, "but you have been so kind." Her little boy was living in Texas with family, and he was very sick. "I know they will starve out there," she added with dramatic flair. If she could just get them all back to New York, everything would be fine. "I am asking a great deal Mr. Huntington but you are the only friend I have in the world," she begged.

Belle soon landed on the shores of the moneyed class as a railroad magnate's paramour and, years later, his wife. Even so, the striver's journey had only just begun. Belle traveled annually to Europe and studied world maps. She toured museums, consulted art experts, and frequented luxury shops. She became a renowned connoisseur, collecting masterpieces by Rembrandt, Frans Hals, and Vermeer.

Belle read deeply and "omnivorously" to keep abreast of current affairs. "She would be a great leader in society," one newspaper stated, "but for her delicate health."

Her self-improvement efforts—as well as prodigal spending on houses, clothing, and jewels—made Belle a sophisticate of the highest rank. It was a journey painstakingly mapped out over many years.

Henry Huntington

Five wooden crates traveled by rail from Broad
Street, New York, to San Marino, California, in the
spring of 1919. The special delivery came from
the East Coast offices of Henry Huntington straight
to his ranch via a Pacific Electric spur line he
had built. Blueprints, rolled linen drawings, and
charts filled each box to the brim—essential
sources the metropolitan kingpin used to map and
plot and plan.

Huntington applied as much fierce tenacity to
shaping Los Angeles as he did to mapping his career.
His revered uncle, rail baron Collis P. Huntington,
was the North Star by which the younger Huntington
charted his life course.

In 1870, at age twenty, the nephew traveled from
small-town Oneonta in upstate New York to Manhattan,
where Collis lived. He took a clerical job to pay the
bills and prove his worth to his fabulously wealthy
relative. His uncle soon sent him to manage a West
Virginia sawmill. The nephew passed the test.

Over the next thirty years, Huntington the younger
supervised railroads all across the country under
Collis's flinty watch. He inherited a fortune of
many millions in 1900, upon Collis's death. "I feel
that everything I am," Huntington later reflected,
"is all due to Collis P."

His uncle proved a thorough and cagey mentor. The
nephew learned his lessons well. Huntington put
a gargantuan inheritance to good use, pouring money
into Southern California, a place he considered
poised for greatness, a "heaven on earth."

Maps were a passion for Huntington, his secretary
Emma Quigley remarked. It made sense. For the
Southern California city builder, they described
the realities of what existed and the promise of what
might be.

New Map of Europe
Fast Takes Form

—Los Angeles Times,
March 4, 1919

It is easier to wage war
than peace.

—Georges Clemenceau,
speech at Verdun, July 20, 1919

It would take a huge monograph to
contain an analysis of all the
types of map forgeries that
the war and the Peace
Conference called forth.

. . .

A map was as good
as a brilliant
poster.

—Isaiah Bowman, American
Geographical Society, reflecting on
the 1919 Paris Peace Conference

FACING
Mount Wilson Observatory, *G58 M8,
N.G.C. 6523, "Sagittarius," Irregular
Nebula, Exposure 3 hrs., 60-inch
Reflector, June 27, 1919* (detail), gelatin
silver print, 8 x 7 ¾ in.

INSERT
(front) *Henry E. Huntington* (detail),
1871, tintype; (back) *Arabella
(Yarrington) Huntington as a Teenager*
(detail), ca. 1865, tintype. Courtesy
of The Hispanic Society of America,
New York

30

18781 Clemenceau, Wilson and Lloyd George Leaving
Palace of Versailles After Signing
Peace Treaty.

Keystone View Company
MANUFACTURERS   COPYRIGHTED MADE IN U.S.A.   PUBLISHERS

Meadville, Pa., New York, N.Y., Portland, Oregon, London, Eng., Sydney, Aus.

18781

LEAVING PALACE OF VERSAILLES

SERIES	75	100	200	300
POSITION	67	90	183	281

Here we have the privilege of meeting face to face three of the most distinguished men of the age, three men whose acts will influence the destinies of millions of men, of all races and of every clime—Clemenceau, President Wilson and Lloyd George.

Clemenceau, "the Tiger of France," is in the foreground, on the left, an indomitable spirit, who kept alive the spirit of France in her darkest days; Lloyd George, Prime Minister of England, the son of a Welsh miner, who rose from the humblest beginnings to the position of the greatest influence in the British Empire, is the man shaking hands at the right. President Wilson, educator, governor, and finally president of the greatest and most powerful republic in the world, we recognize at a glance.

These men have just come from a momentous occasion—the signing of the Peace Treaty at Versailles, an occasion at which the fate of millions yet unborn was determined by the stroke of a pen. Notables from all nations are about them, but these three men are the cynosure of all eyes. See them in the back row straining forward to follow with their eyes the progress of these three. And countless thousands are in front, packed around the gates of this ancient palace of Louis XIV, to greet them. The civilized world is on tiptoe for this occasion, for it brings to a close the most terrific and bloodiest war the world has ever seen, a war fought in the air, on land, on the sea and under its waters; a war which cost the lives of 8,000,000 men, wrecked millions of homes, and destroyed property beyond computation.

Copyright by The Keystone View Company

ABOVE
Keystone View Co., *Clemenceau, Wilson, and Lloyd George Leaving Palace of Versailles after Signing Peace Treaty*, June 28, 1919, from World War through the Stereoscope, gelatin silver print (recto and verso), 3 ½ x 7 in.

FOLLOWING SPREAD
Sir Douglas Haig, *Despatches (December 1915–April 1919)*, 1919, E. P. Dutton & Co., New York

The map on the following spread traces the movement of the British army into Germany's Rhineland and the city of Cologne. Their journey began with surrender on November 11, 1918, and ended about a month later. The dark lines indicate slow-moving infantry, whereas the bright lines show the advance of faster-moving cavalry. The deteriorating economic and political situation in Germany meant that the Allied armies were needed to provide stability.

102

Maps miniaturize the world, pressing its irregularities flat and making it seem manageable. They are realistic and pragmatic—showing topography, rivers, coasts, and boundaries—the world as it is. But they are also places to dream about the world to come.

At the Paris Peace Conference, maps were key. From January to June 1919, delegates quarreled over reparations and blamed the war on the Germans, but it was the land and the people represented by the maps that really counted. The Council of Four—Woodrow Wilson (United States), Georges Clemenceau (France), David Lloyd George (United Kingdom), and Vittorio Orlando (Italy)—divvied up German colonies in Africa and the Pacific among the Allies. The long-suppressed Czechs, Slovaks, Poles, Lithuanians, Latvians, and Estonians jockeyed successfully to establish independent nations from remnants of the German, Austro-Hungarian, and Russian empires.

The delegates also ironed out the details of the League of Nations, a proto–United Nations designed to peacefully resolve disputes. The League realized the fourteenth of Wilson's Fourteen Points, a set of principles and objectives that guided him in his quest to secure a lasting peace. The city of Geneva greeted its selection as the site for the League's permanent secretariat with pride, as this proclamation in French shows.

Not every mapping project that year fought over boundaries. With lines and ovals, geneticists diagrammed dominant and recessive traits of eye color in flies (p. 107). Albert Henry Munsell used his photometer to break color into identifiable units and standardize color description for medicine, geology, botany, and other fields (pp. 114–15).

As the quotation referenced earlier reminds us, "A map was as good as a brilliant poster" for hawking a political idea, no matter how despicable. The colorful maps in Lothrop Stoddard's *The Rising Tide of Color against White World-Supremacy* underscore the author's

February 26, 1919—
Grand Canyon becomes the United States' fifteenth national park.

February 1919—
Candidates to the first Pan-African Congress meet in Paris to protest the exclusion of Africans from Paris Peace Conference deliberations.

May 29, 1919—
British scientist Arthur Eddington confirms Albert Einstein's theory of general relativity during a total solar eclipse.

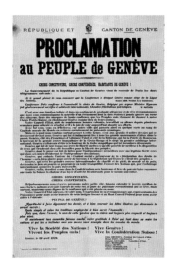

Proclamation au Peuple de Genève,
April 29, 1919, broadside,
31 ½ x 20 ½ in., L. Gilbert, Geneva,
Switzerland

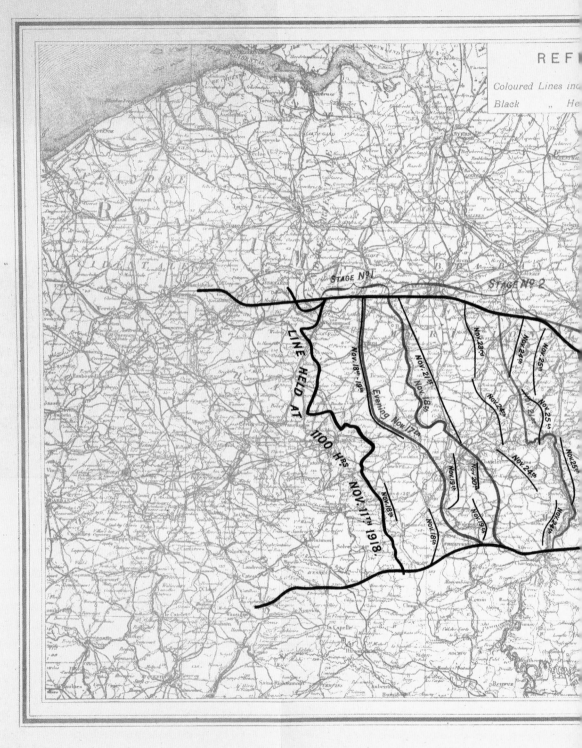

REF

Coloured Lines ind

Black   " He

STAGE Nº 1

STAGE Nº 2

LINE HELD AT 1100 HRS NOV. 11TH 1918.

Nov. 18th-19th

Evening Nov. 17th

Nov. 21st

Nov. 18th

Nov. 23rd

Nov. 24th

Nov. 25th

Nov. 24th

Nov. 25th

Nov. 18th

Nov. 19th

Nov. 20th

Nov. 24th

Nov. 25th

Nov. 19th

Nov. 24th

Nov. 18th

Miles 10   5   0   10   20

Kilometres 20   10   0   20   40

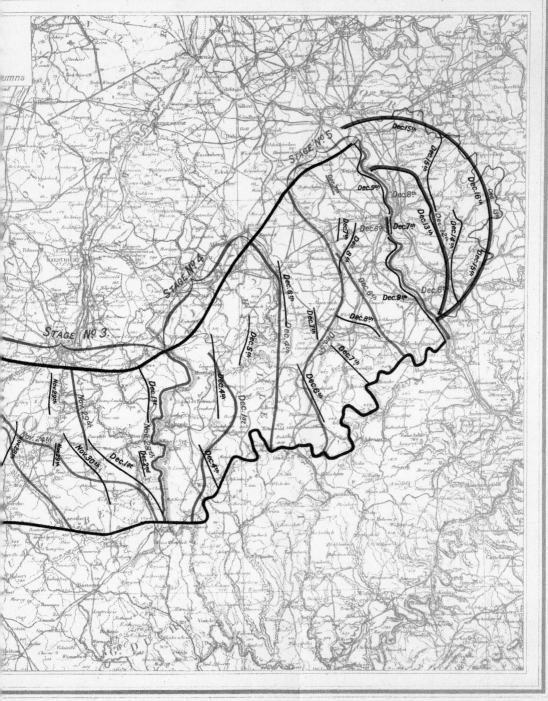

Ordnance Survey, 1919

50   60   70   80   90 Miles

80   100   120   140 Kilometres

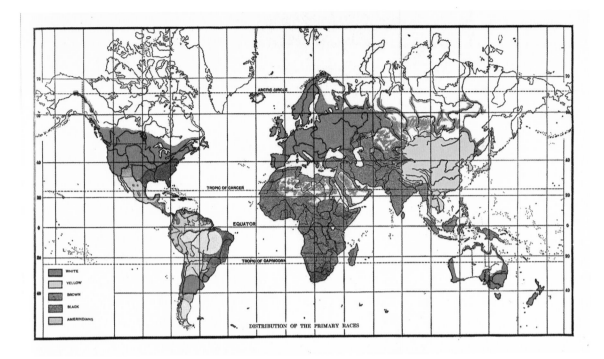

DISTRIBUTION OF THE PRIMARY RACES

WHITE
YELLOW
BROWN
BLACK
AMERINDIANS

June 28, 1919—
Covenant of the
League of Nations
is signed at the
Paris Peace
Conference.
The United States
does not join.

November 19, 1919—
U.S. Senate rejects
the Treaty of
Versailles, marking a
turn to isolationism.

paranoid claims about the white race's precarious position. His books about the connection between race and achievement were widely admired in the 1920s and later by Nazi propagandist Alfred Rosenberg.

While some mapped the globe, others charted the stars. Astronomers at the Mount Wilson Observatory near Pasadena peered into the cosmos with their recently completed 100-inch Hooker telescope, then the world's largest (pp. 132–33). On September 15, 1919, Francis G. Pease pointed its lens to the waning moon's bumpy surface and captured images of striking detail. Though astronomers had been using photography since shortly after its invention in 1839, Pease's lunar photographs were the first of sufficient resolution to be more accurate than looking through the telescope's eyepiece and drawing. Also in 1919, a team at Mount Wilson installed the first astronomical interferometer, an

Map

instrument that enabled Pease and Albert A. Michelson to determine that the supergiant star Betelgeuse was seven hundred times the size of the sun.

When they were not gazing upward, the astronomers on Mount Wilson might have looked down to see the effects of Los Angeles's swelling population, and the scramble to manage and profit from this growth. In Laura Whitlock's map of Los Angeles, the radiating circles centered on downtown forecast expansion into the hinterlands (p. 124). The Los Angeles Railway recorded population density, a dot at a time, to show recently completed buildings adjacent to transit routes (p. 118). One cannot help but fill in the empty space with today's gridded carpet of homes, businesses, and factories.

A group called the Fifth Street Association commissioned plans for a string of neoclassical public buildings— a library, art gallery, and auditorium—architectural monuments meant to outshine those of Eastern cities (pp. 122–23). The association's fantasy of turning Fifth Street into a truncated Parisian boulevard would never materialize. Then, as now, Los Angeles's built environment flouts the rules of good taste—creeping, sprawling, and sprouting whichever way the market takes it.

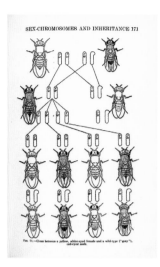

ABOVE
"Cross between a yellow, white-eyed female and a wild-type ('gray') red-eyed male," in Thomas Hunt Morgan, *The Physical Basis of Heredity*, 1919, J. B. Lippincott, Philadelphia

FACING
"Distribution of the Primary Races," in Lothrop Stoddard, *The Rising Tide of Color against White World-Supremacy*, 1920, C. Scribner's Sons, New York

Map　　　107

Lawrence of Arabia

As a young British army officer, T. E. Lawrence (1888–1935) collaborated with the Hashemite clan, who controlled Mecca, to wage guerrilla warfare against the Ottoman Turks during World War I. The Ottomans had sided with the Germans, and the British sought to topple them. Lawrence became well known for blowing up trains and railways and for his photogenic, romanticized presentation in a keffiyeh headdress. After the war, Lawrence learned of Britain's plans to divide the Middle East with France at the Paris Peace Conference. He advised King Hussein to dispatch his son Faisal to represent Hejaz, their kingdom along the Red Sea in what is now Saudi Arabia. Lawrence accompanied Faisal at the conference, serving as his translator, and he also began drafting *The Seven Pillars of Wisdom*, his first-hand account of the Arabs' struggle against the Ottomans. On May 18, he left the conference, angry that a sovereign pan-Arab nation would not be established. He began a circuitous air journey to Cairo that began badly when his plane crash-landed in Rome, killing the pilot and copilot and seriously injuring Lawrence. After the crash, he penned a witty and understated letter of thanks to Frederick Daw, who had extricated him from the wreckage.

T. E. Lawrence with Auda abu Tayi, Leader of the Howeitat Tribe, in the Desert, 1917, gelatin silver print, 6 ⅜ x 4 ⅜ in.

RIGHT
T. E. Lawrence, Letter to Frederick Daw, July 5, 1919, Cairo; (inserted) Lawrence's penknife, which also survived the crash

FOLLOWING SPREAD
The delegation from Hejaz to the Paris Peace Conference shows Prince Faisal with delegates and advisers (left to right) Rustem Haidar, Brigadier General Nuri Said, Captain Pisani of France, Lawrence, and Hassan Kadri; the man behind them is known only as Salem, January 22, 1919, gelatin silver print, 3 ½ x 5 ½ in.

CENTRAL AIR COMMUNICATION STATION,

ROYAL AIR FORCE, BASRA,

MESOPOTAMIA.

From :- O.C.,

Central Air Communication Station,

Basra, Mesopotamia.

236766 A.C.2. Daw F.J.

To whom it may concern:-

This is to certify that the above mentioned airman took an active part in No.58 Squadron's flight from France to Egypt, May - June 1919. - the first longest flight of its kind.

Unfortunately the machine in which he was flying as mechanic was crashed in an accident at Rome and both pilots being killed. Although very shaken and hurt A.C.2.Daw did much to render assistance to the other occupants of the aeroplane; one of which was Colonel T.C.Lawrence C.B.,D.S.O., etc., who informed me later and especially commended on the excellent way A.C.2. Daw went about this work.

He is leaving me for demobilization and to take up his civilian employment again.

Capt.
Commanding C.A.C.S.,R.A.F.

Central Air Communication Station, Royal Air Force, Basra,
Letter "To Whom it May Concern" commending
Frederick J. Daw for saving T. E. Lawrence's life,
October 3, 1919, typescript letter and tape

Map

109

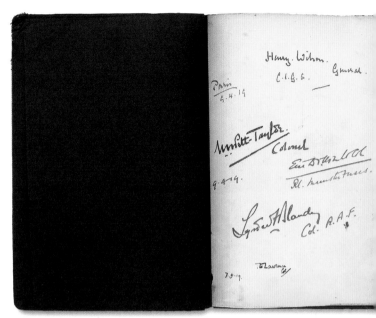

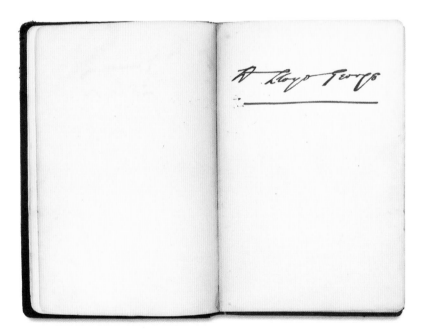

ABOVE AND FACING
Pages from T. E. Lawrence's Paris Peace
Conference autograph album,
7 ½ x 5 in. each

Map

The album includes the signatures of such luminaries as British prime minister David Lloyd George, Field Marshal Edmund Allenby, whom Lawrence had fought alongside in the Middle East, and Deputy First Sea Lord George P. Hope.

Map

113

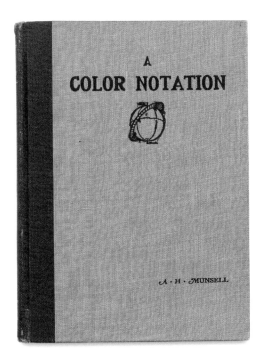

Mapping Color

Albert Henry Munsell (1858–1918) studied painting
in Boston and then in Paris during the 1880s, and
for a time taught color theory to art students. In his
book *A Color Notation*, first published in 1905, he
divided the spectrum into five principal hues: red,
purple, blue, green, and yellow. He then organized
the hues by chroma and lightness. Chroma refers to
the brightness or purity of a color—the intensity of
redness or blueness, for instance—whereas lightness,
or value, reflects how much white has been added.
In the "Middle Color Scales" chart, bright red, R 5/10,
appears at the top. This pure red is then grayed
out step by step—that is, its chroma is reduced.
This guide to color was among the very first issued
by Munsell's company after it opened in 1917. With
some refinements, the system that Munsell invented
continues to be used in fields like botany and geology
to describe colors in a systematic way.

Map

PLATE I

A BALANCED COLOR SPHERE
PASTEL SKETCH

A COLOR NOTATION

BY

A. H. MUNSELL

AN ILLUSTRATED SYSTEM DEFINING ALL COLORS AND
THEIR RELATIONS BY MEASURED
SCALES OF

Hue, Value, and Chroma

MADE IN SOLID PAINT FOR THE ACCOMPANYING

Color Atlas

INTRODUCTION BY H. E. CLIFFORD

Fifth Edition, Revised and Enlarged.

MUNSELL COLOR COMPANY
BOSTON
1919

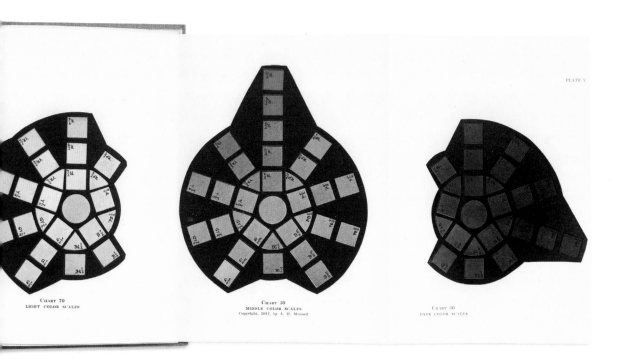

PLATE V

CHART 70
LIGHT COLOR SCALES

CHART 50
MIDDLE COLOR SCALES
Copyright, 1911, by A. H. Munsell

CHART 30
DARK COLOR SCALES

ABOVE AND FACING
Albert Henry Munsell, *A Color Notation*, 1919,
Munsell Color Co., Boston

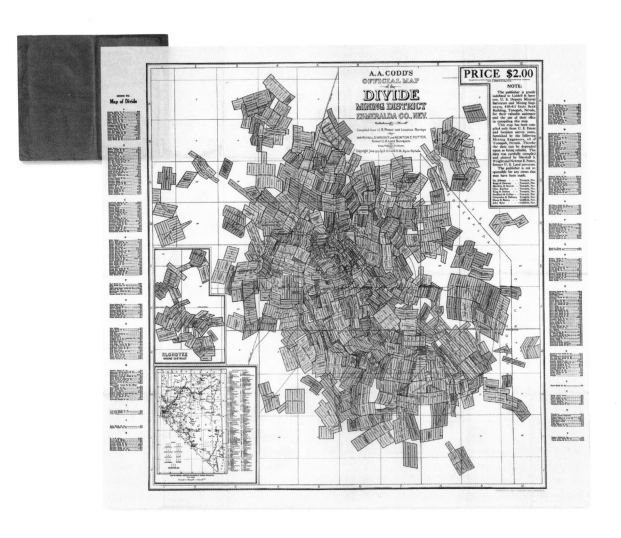

Charles P. Eager, Marshall S. Wright, and Newton E. Potter, *A. A. Codd's Official Map of the Divide Mining District* (and detail), Esmeralda Co., Nevada, 1919, lithograph, 30 x 37 in., Commercial Art Co., San Francisco

In the spring of 1919, miners discovered a silver-bearing lode in Esmeralda County, Nevada, that set off a prospecting frenzy. This map's colorful mosaic of mineral-rights claims documents the more than three hundred companies formed in the rush. At least eighty mine shafts were dug that summer, and electrical lines were strung into power mining equipment. The yields proved smaller than estimated, and the excitement quickly dissipated.

Map

117

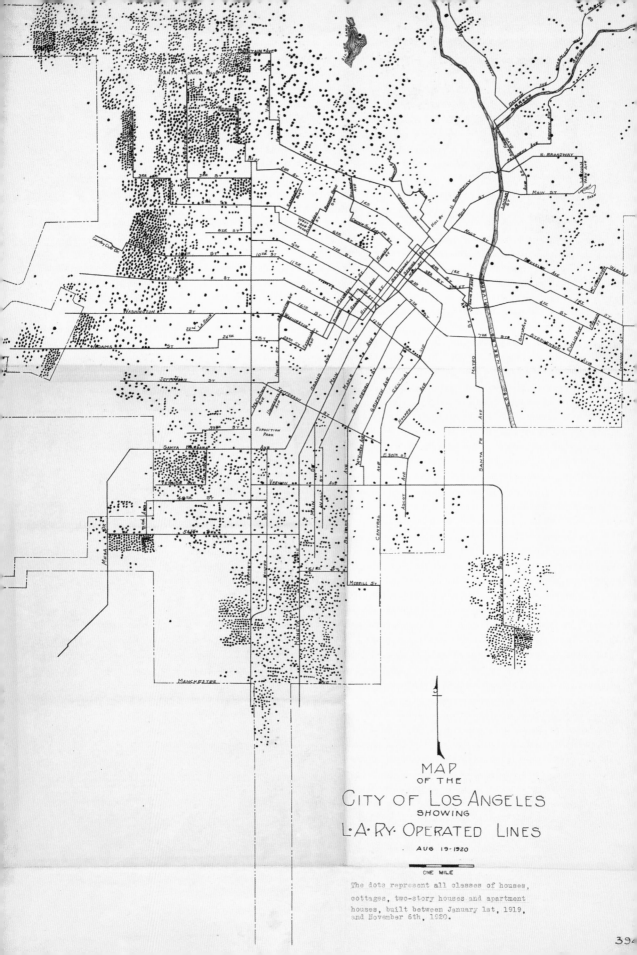

MAP
OF THE
CITY OF LOS ANGELES
SHOWING
L·A·RY· OPERATED LINES

AUG 19·1920

ONE MILE

The dots represent all classes of houses,
cottages, two-story houses and apartment
houses, built between January 1st, 1919,
and November 6th, 1920.

394

Los Angeles Maps Itself

As the twentieth century began, Henry Huntington bought up giant swaths of Southern California land and laid mile after mile of track in every direction. Suburban development followed. He adhered to the principle of anticipatory growth: if you build it, they will come. Come, they did. Towns and suburbs soon filled in his transit-driven grid, and Huntington's land rose in value because he could bring water, power, and trolleys to it. This growth formula, and the racially restrictive covenants and practices placed atop those myriad real estate plots, drove development in greater Los Angeles. More than any other single individual, Huntington helped define the shape, boundaries, and demographics of what became a sprawling regional map. From 1900 to 1919, the population of Los Angeles County increased by an astounding 450 percent.

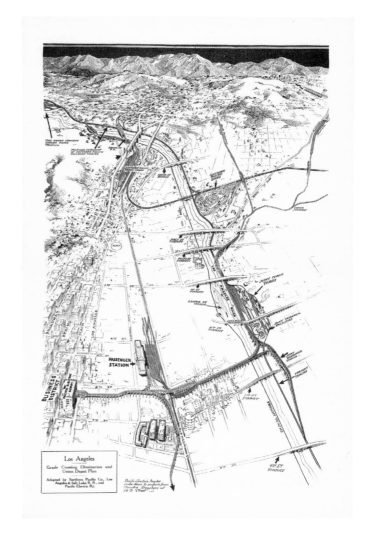

RIGHT
"Los Angeles Grade Crossing Elimination and Union Depot Plan," in *The Pacific Electric Magazine*, March 10, 1919, Pacific Electric Railway Company, Los Angeles

FACING
The caption for a map produced by the Los Angeles Railway says: "The dots represent all classes of houses, cottages, two-story houses and apartment houses, built between January 1st, 1919, and November 6th, 1920." Los Angeles Railway Corp., *Map of the City of Los Angeles Showing Los Angeles Railway Operated Lines*, August 19, 1920, ink on blueline print (reprographic copy), 24 ⅛ x 16 ¼ in.

Map

119

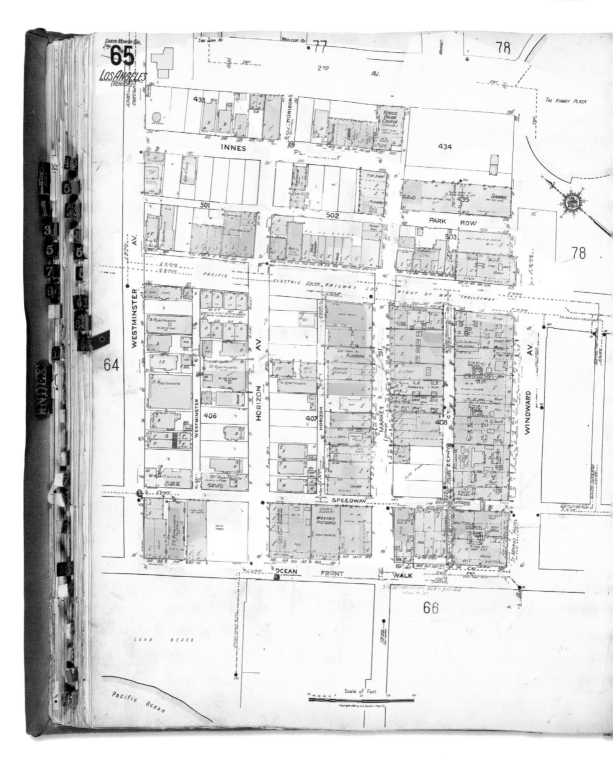

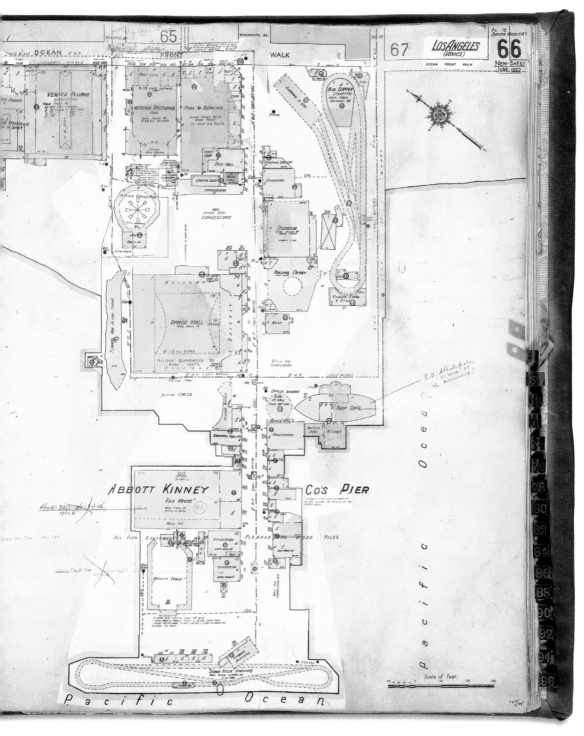

View of Abbott [*sic*] Kinney Pier, Venice,
California, in *Insurance Maps of Santa
Monica Including Venice, California,*
1918/1919, Sanborn Map
Co., New York

Map

121

PERSPECTIVE VIEW:—Of these Library and Auditorium buildings, is shown owing page, and as has been mentioned in the text, are designed in the classic chitecture as being a style more appropriate to their architectural dignity pressive of the purposes for which these buildings are to be used.

LIBRARY:—As will be seen by reference to the block plan of this building, the map, there are four large, rectangular interior light courts, each court 80' 0" x 80' 0",—or some 6400 square feet of area. The of each of these courts, considering the height of the building, will be ample size to insure perfect lighting and natural ventilation for all parts of

the interior of the building, including of course, the large three-storied Memorial Hall that extends through the building from Olive Street to Grand Avenue.

This Library Building has been fully described in the text, both as to its plan and general dimensions, as well as its cost of construction.

THE AUDITORIUM:—This building, as shown by the block-plan, and also in the perspective, faces upon the proposed "straight-through" extension of Fifth Street, and instead of having the Choral Hall and the Art Gallery buildings joined together as a part of one building and similar to the Auditorium in San Francisco, with its smaller banqueting and choral halls,—we have separated these buildings and then joined them

by means of connecting galleries, as shown in the block plan. In this manne buildings have an abundance of light and air on all sides thereof.

This permits of much more utilization of outer wall space, or office space at all permissible in San Francisco. In that Auditorium building almost ev foot of space is utilized and is rented out almost continuously through the standard rate of rental as fixed by city ordinance.

The San Francisco main auditorium is 200' 0" wide by 187' 0" deep, about 5500 on the main floor and about 5000 in the gallery, whereas the pl proposed Los Angeles Auditorium shows the main auditorium as being 196' 0

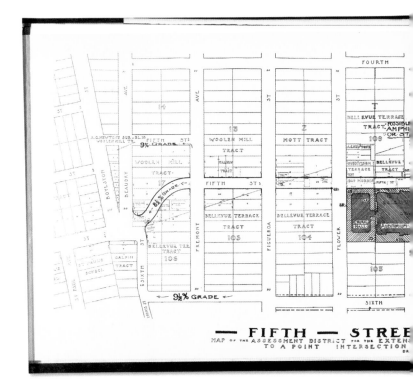

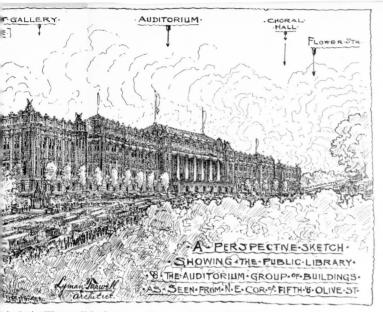

GALLERY.   ·AUDITORIUM·   ·CHORAL· HALL·   FLOWER·STR·

·A·PERSPECTIVE·SKETCH·
·SHOWING·THE·PUBLIC·LIBRARY·
·&·THE·AUDITORIUM·GROUP·OF·BUILDINGS·
·AS·SEEN·FROM·N·E·COR·OF·FIFTH·&·OLIVE·ST·

Lyman Farwell
architect

LEFT
Lyman Farwell, "A Perspective Sketch Showing the Public Library and the Auditorium Group of Buildings as seen from the N.E. Corner of Fifth & Olive Street"

BELOW
Paul C. Pape, "Map of the Assessment District for the Extension of Fifth Street West from Grand Avenue," October 1, 1919

Both in *Copy of Preliminary Description, Maps, and Sketches of Proposed Civic Centers for the City of Los Angeles, California,* December 1919, Temple Block Civic Center League and Fifth Street Association, Los Angeles

nd seating about 9000 persons, with the gallery as accommodating
y when final plans for this Auditorium building are completed the
building that will not seat over about 10,000, or possibly 12,000 per-
s mentioned in the text of this report.
r walls, ceilings and other architectural effects of this proposed
properly constructed of sound-absorbing material and a better and
rd for acoustic principles there is every reason to be absolutely
uaranteed that this building can be built not only perfect in all its

constructive and accoustical details, but that it can, in a reasonable bonding period of
time, be made to pay not only for its cost of construction, but also for the cost of the
land it is to occupy as well.
 This Auditorium building might likewise, in course of time thus also pay for the
cost of the Art Gallery and the Choral Hall that are logical adjuncts to the Auditorium,
and particularly to this proposed "Art and Cultural" Civic Center.

THE FIFTH STREET EXTENSION AND ART AND CULTURAL CENTER:

THE MAP ON THIS PAGE:—Showing the cutting through of Fifth Street, from the junction of Boylston Street and Beaudry Avenue on the Sixth Street Hill to Grand Avenue,—also shows a possible location for the Public Library and the Public Auditorium group of buildings that form the proposed Art and Cultural Center," that has been more fully described in the text.

This proposed opening up of Fifth Street is primarily intended to form an auxiliary thoroughfare for the traffic coming into the business center of the city from the west, north and south. Not one of the established cross street gradings will be disturbed and the steepest part of the grade, from Fremont Street southwesterly by means of the curved portion of this proposed new thoroughfare is an 8½% grade, compared to the 9½% grade of Sixth Street from Figueroa and Fremont up the Sixth Street Hill.

It will also be noticed that the natural grade in front of the proposed Auditorium buildings will be but 1.7% and that the present circuitous route from the corner of Fifth and Fremont Streets via the so-called northerly and detached Fifth Street to Beaudry Avenue is a 9% grade.

The ever-increasing traffic from the west and the south, as well as the north, is demanding attention and some practical recognition and an efficient settlement.

The tortuous winding grading grade down the Sixth Street Hill with its sharp turn at Loomis Street is becoming more and more a dangerous menace as well as an expensive and inefficient entrance for a growing section of the city to the business center.

Furthermore it would not only be impractical to "contour" Fifth Street around the southerly end of the Normal Hill site, but an inefficient and useless expense as well.

As has been mentioned in the text and on account of the barrenlike north wall of the Bible Institute, as well as for other reasons therein enumerated, it will be far more practical to extend Fifth Street through to Grand Avenue in a straight line as shown on the map, and have the Auditorium buildings front upon this new and practically even graded Fifth Street.

This Fifth Street proposition though comparatively inexpensive as compared to other proposed civic undertakings, has already been arranged for and the assessment district apportioned off to provide for the expense of the undertaking with practically no expense to the city at large.

Some day the hillside opposite the Auditorium may be utilized for a large open-air amphitheater, as noted on the map,—and the Auditorium and its annex-buildings, the Art Gallery and Choral Hall, are designed with reference to form a fitting and attractive background to such an amphitheater.

The cost of the lands and other property, as well as the cost of grading, involved in this Fifth Street extension proposition, will amount to about $200,000.00.

Map   123

OFFICIAL TRANSPORTATION
AND
CITY MAP OF LOS ANGELES CALIFORNIA AND SUBURB

Laura L. Whitlock, Cartographer

The *Official Transportation and City Map of Los Angeles*—on its seventh edition by 1919—was the work of Laura Whitlock (1862–1934), official cartographer of Los Angeles County and the nation's only woman map publisher at the time. In Whitlock's rendering, circles indicate radial distances from downtown, a green border defines familiar city limits, and yellow and red lines trace the Los Angeles Railway and Pacific Electric streetcar systems. Between 1873 and the 1940s, Huntington's interurban railways catalyzed the region's rapid growth, transforming areas like Boyle Heights, Hollywood, and Pasadena into accessible suburbs. Whitlock constructed her biggest maps, like the one shown here, from multiple plates that she then compiled and printed for the mass market. Her plans were so popular that pirated copies abounded; she sued for copyright infringement and won the country's first-ever such court case in 1913.

FACING
Laura L. Whitlock, *Official Transportation and City Map of Los Angeles, California, and Suburbs* (detail), ca. 1919, 50 x 38 in.

FOLLOWING SPREADS
Pacific Electric Company, *Valuation Section No. 64, Pacific Electric Railway Map of Pasadena Short Line* (South Pasadena details), ca. 1914–45, pen, ink, and pencil on linen, 37 x 492 in.

The details on the following spreads are extracted from a thirty-seven-foot-long, hand-drawn linen map, one of dozens of such scrolls drafted by the Engineering Department of the Pacific Electric Company. These maps served as the company's master or "vault" copies, with additions and redactions painstakingly recorded over time. They are extraordinary documents of land ownership and infrastructural detail along every inch of the Pacific Electric line, a meticulous recounting of the ways in which Henry Huntington's transportation and real estate empire defined and shaped the region.

Map

125

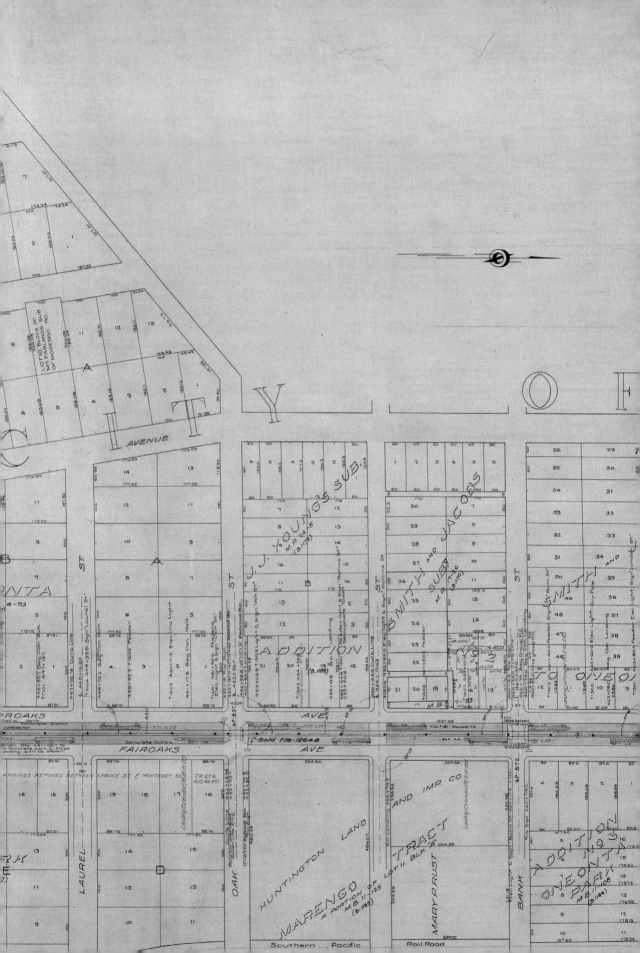

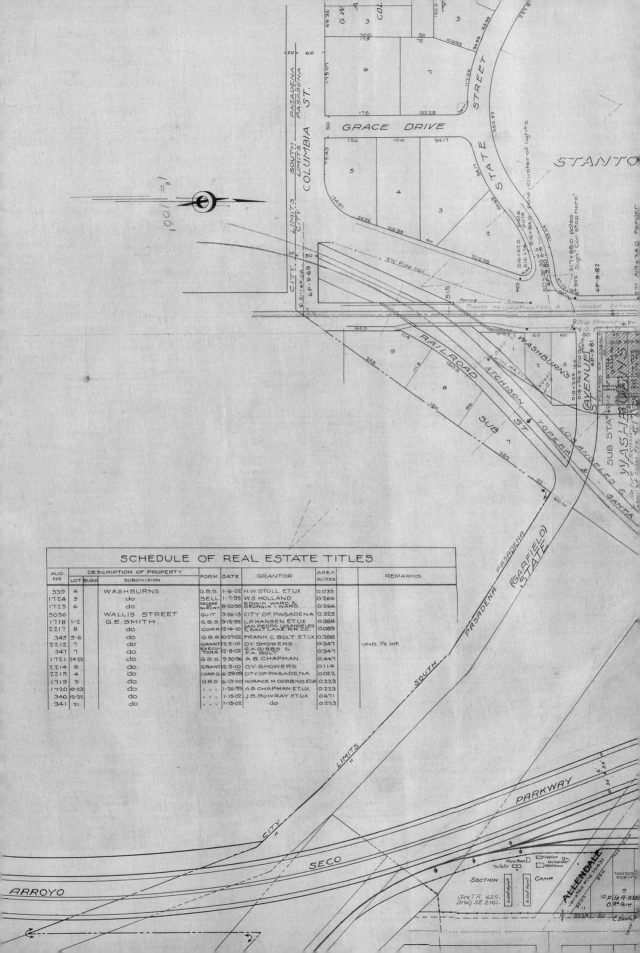

SCHEDULE OF REAL ESTATE TITLES

AUD. No	DESCRIPTION OF PROPERTY			FORM	DATE	GRANTOR	AREA ACRES	REMARKS
	LOT	BLOCK	SUBDIVISION					
339	4		WASHBURNS	G.B.S	1-6-02	H.W. STOLL ETUX	0.033	
1724	5		do	SELL	1-7-95	W.S. HOLLAND	0.266	
1725	6		do	DECREE SUP.CRT	8-20-95	EDWIN WARD & GEORGIA T. WARD	0.266	
5056	1-2		WALLIS STREET	QUIT	3-26-13	CITY OF PASADENA	0.325	
1718	1-2		G.E. SMITH	G.B.S	9-15-95	L.P. HANSEN ET.UX	0.388	
2217	8		do	CORP.R	12-16-10	SAN PEDRO LOS ANGELES & SALT LAKE R.R CO	0.089	
345	5-6		do	G.B.S	10-27-02	FRANK C. BOLT ET.UX	0.388	
2212	7		do	GRANT	2-5-10	O.V. SHOWERS	0.347	
347	7		do	EXECUTORS	12-8-02	G.A. GIBBS & F.A. BOLT	0.347	UND. 1/2 int.
1721	24-25		do	G.B.S	9-30-96	A.B. CHAPMAN	0.447	
2214	8		do	GRANT	2-5-10	O.V. SHOWERS	0.114	
2215	4		do	CORP.G	6-29-09	CITY OF PASADENA	0.022	
1719	9		do	G.B.S	6-13-00	HORACE M. DOBBINS ETUX	0.223	
1720	10-23		do	. . .	1-26-99	A.B. CHAPMAN ET.UX.	0.223	
340	12-22		do	. . .	1-15-02	J.B. ROWRAY ET.UX	0.671	
341	21		do	. . .	1-15-02	do	0.223	

α_{1920} $10^h 42^m 21^s$ α_{1860} $10^h 39^m 10^s$ $+3.19$ N.G.C. 3367
δ $+ 14° 10'.2$ npd. $75° 30'.9$ $+18''.9$ G.C. 2193
                                                                                                                      H II 78 Leonis
Trans 2/6/14 $\beta B, cL, iR, vg16M, r, 1^{st}g3.$ h 748
                                                                                                                      $\beta + 59°$ 1200°

                                                                                                                      $D'H_{1,2,}$
                                                                                                                      Lo Rosse
                                                                                                                      Schmidt
                                                                                                                      Schonfeld,
                                                                                                                      Schultz
                                                                                                                      Vogel$_2$

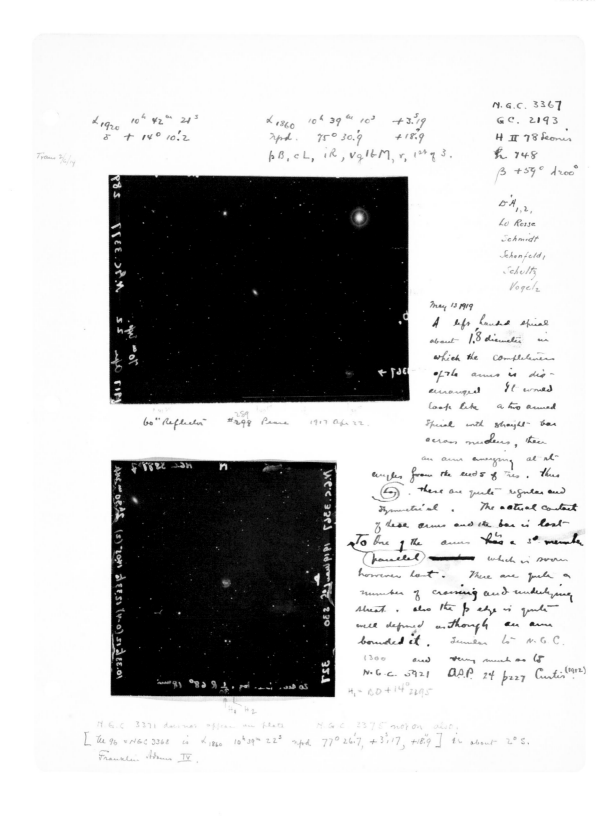

60" Reflector   #298 Pease   1917 Apr. 22.

May 13 1919

A left handed spiral about 1'.8 diameter in which the completeness of the arms is disarranged. It would look like a two armed spiral with straight bar across nucleus, then an arm emerging at at- angles from the ends of these, thus ⟲. there are quite regular and symmetrical. The actual content of these arms and the bar is lost. To one of the arms has a 3° member (parallel) ——— which is soon however lost. There are quite a number of crossing and underlying streak. also the β edge is quite well defined as though an arm bounded it. Similar to N.G.C. 1300 and very much as (5 N.G.C. 5921 A.S.P. 24 p227 Curtis (1912). $H_1 = BD + 14° 2295$

N.G.C. 3371 does not appear on plate.   N.G.C. 2375 not on also.
[the 9b = NGC 3368 is α_{1860} $10^h 39^m 22^s$ npd. $77° 26'.7$, $+3'.17$, $+18''.9$] it about 2°S.
Franklin Adams IV.

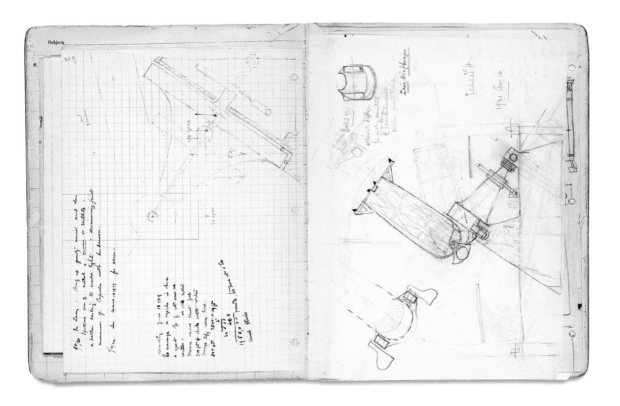

(above) Francis G. Pease played a role in the technical problem-solving around construction and installation of the Mount Wilson telescope. On the left side of this haphazardly assembled notebook are notes from June 1919 that appear to calculate the mass of a telescope component filled with water. The component is sketched in pencil at top. The weight proved excessive, and Pease wrote, "too much wt [weight] and too much strain."

(facing) Francis G. Pease, Notes and photographs related to spiral nebulae as seen through a telescope at the Mount Wilson Solar Observatory, 1917–19. Two photographs and notes about N.G.C. 3367, a spiral galaxy in the constellation of Leo Major. Top image taken April 12, 1917; bottom image taken March 1, 1919

Ad Astra

In the early twentieth century, Los Angeles became a place of astronomical discovery. Mount Wilson Observatory's two telescopes, 60 and 100 inches in diameter, peered into the universe. The 100-inch was the world's largest from 1917 to 1941. The photographs from the papers of Francis G. Pease (1881–1938), an astronomer at Mount Wilson who collaborated with Edwin Hubble, are of well-known heavenly bodies, such as the moon, Halley's Comet, and constellations. Observations of nebulae with these new telescopes proved they were beyond the Milky Way, not stars within it, revealing that the universe was many orders of magnitude larger than presumed.

ABOVE
Head of Halley's Comet, Exposure
8 Min., 60-Inch Reflector, May 5, 1919,
gelatin silver print, 10 ¾ x 15 ¼ in.

FACING
South Central Portion of the Moon at
Last Quarter, Made with the 100-Inch
Reflector (detail), September 15, 1919,
gelatin silver print, 9 ½ x 7 ½ in.

FOLLOWING SPREAD
Total Eclipse of the Sun, June 8, 1918,
lithograph, from a painting by Howard
Russell Butler in *Natural History*
Magazine, March 1919

132

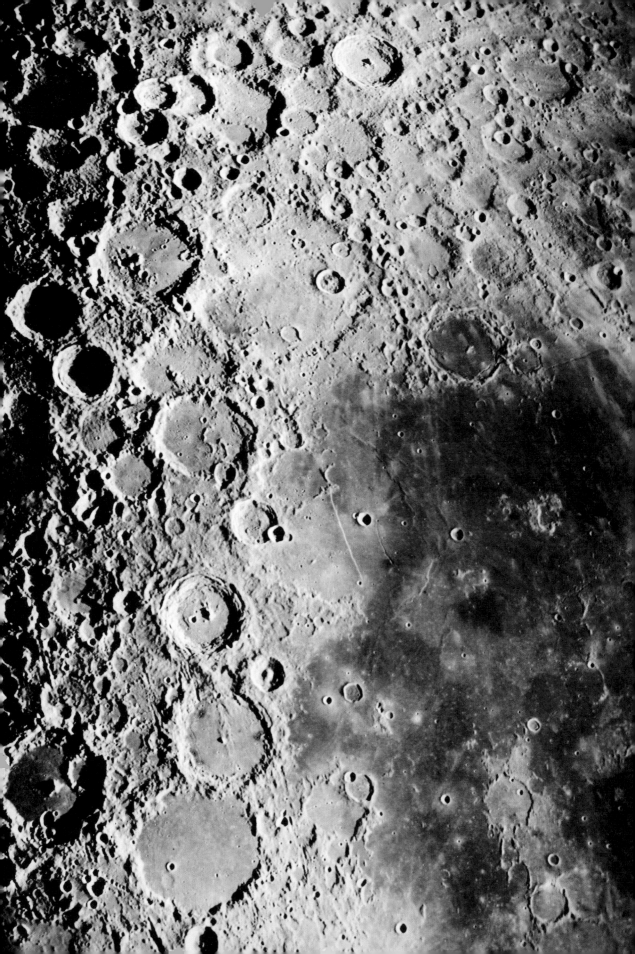

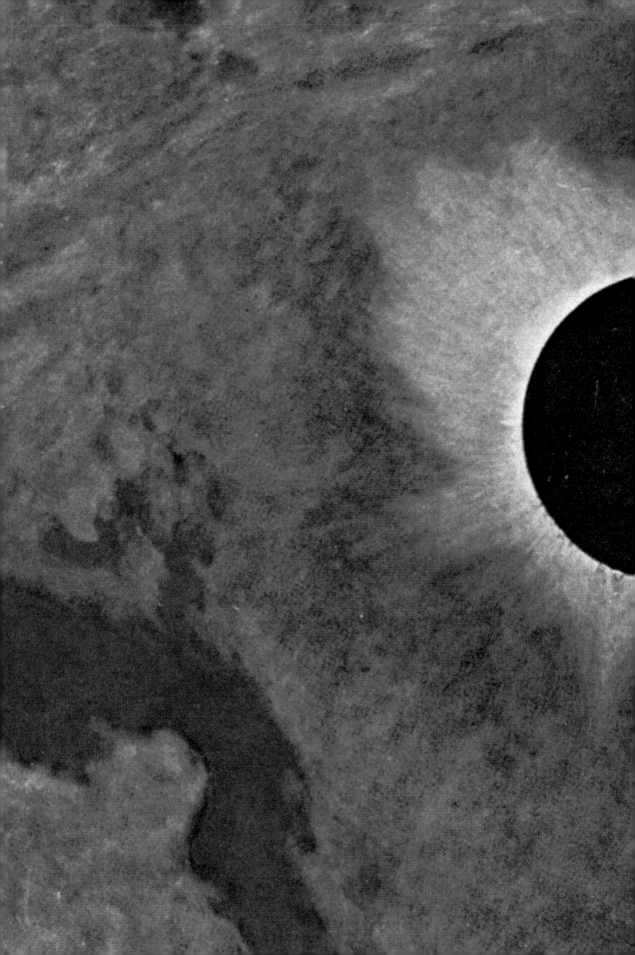

Henry Huntington

Henry Huntington engineered a second fortune over a web of steel rails. In 1901, leveraging an inheritance of millions, he snapped up vast tracts of undeveloped land while expanding the Los Angeles streetcar system and its crisscrossed lines.

He ripped out cables, upgraded passenger cars, and laid a thousand miles of track. The savvy monopolist left nothing to chance. He created the Huntington Land and Improvement Company to oversee his real estate domain. He bought telephone, water, and power companies to guarantee his empire's exponential growth.

He tapped his increasing wealth to buy a tidal wave of books. Literary treasures poured out of Great Britain's estates, bibliographic troves relinquished by aristocrats and noble families down on their luck. The bounty washed into the hands of elite dealers and auctioneers before rushing onward to a status-hungry American clientele. Huntington dominated this latter-day Gilded Age group.

In 1919, Huntington announced what some, including his New York librarians, had begun to suspect. He planned to load the "world's greatest private library" on boxcars—some 120,000 volumes, thirty tons of knowledge—and send it off to the nation's far western shore.

Critics were vocal and opprobrium swift. Why would this parvenu bookman relocate the patrimony of Great Britain and early America thousands of miles from the intellectual centers of the United States? And to Los Angeles, no less. Was he doing it simply because he could? Or was the relocation a pettier act, a nose-thumbing to the East Coast and its hidebound rules?

"None of the above," was Huntington's retort. He owed his millions to California and its people, and he yearned to give them a gift. He loved Los Angeles with a paternal pride. He had championed the region and watched it grow, certain that a still-more-glorious future lay ahead. Establishing his namesake institution in Southern California was an original and audacious move.

Arabella Huntington

Arabella Huntington spent a lifetime on the move. Her restless wandering suggests she was running from something, though it is not clear what.

As a teenager, Belle fled Virginia for New York City at the close of the Civil War. She bounced from the city to New Orleans to Texas and back to Manhattan, where she settled with her young son in 1874.

As Mrs. Collis P. Huntington, she roved between the grandiose properties the pair acquired, including three in New York State: a mansion on Fifth Avenue and 57th Street; an estate called The Homestead, at Throggs Neck overlooking Long Island Sound; and Camp Pine Knot in the Adirondack Mountains on Raquette Lake.

After Collis's death in 1900, her pace only increased. Belle dashed back and forth from New York to Europe, especially France, where she purchased not one, but two, grand mansions.

Belle adored automobiles, and she craved speed. She shipped luxurious town cars—and their chauffeurs—to Europe and back. Her drivers routinely clocked over the speed limit (about twelve miles per hour in the day). Arabella got speeding tickets wherever she went.

When Belle became Mrs. Arabella D. Huntington Huntington in 1913, travel continued to define her life. She and Edward divided the year into thirds: France in the springtime, New York in summer and fall, and usually California in the winter months.

Belle never stayed in one place for long.

1919 ——————— Move

**The opinion is growing all over the
country among traffic officers
and motor car drivers that
there should be some
means of notifying the
driver in "the car
behind" when
the car ahead
is about to
slow up
or stop.**

—"Demand Growing for Auto
Night Signal Device,"
Touring Topics, January 1919

**Of course the present high landing
speed of an aëroplane is the
cause of many accidents.
Thirty-five miles an
hour, except
where the
head
resistance is
great, is the slowest
speed now made in landing
a heavier-than-air machine.**

—Evan J. David, "Commercial Flying:
Business Possibilities of the Aëroplane,"
Saturday Evening Post, January 11, 1919

FACING
J. C. Milligan, *Crowd outside Bullock's
Department Store for August
Clearance Sale, Los Angeles* (detail), 1919,
gelatin silver print, 10 x 13 in.

INSERT
(front, left to right) *Henry E. Huntington,
Robert Burdette, unidentified driver,
Clara Burdette, and Harry Chandler at
the Mission Inn, Riverside*, ca. 1910,
gelatin silver print; (back) Felix Nadar,
Arabella Huntington, ca. 1903.
Courtesy of The Hispanic Society of
America, New York

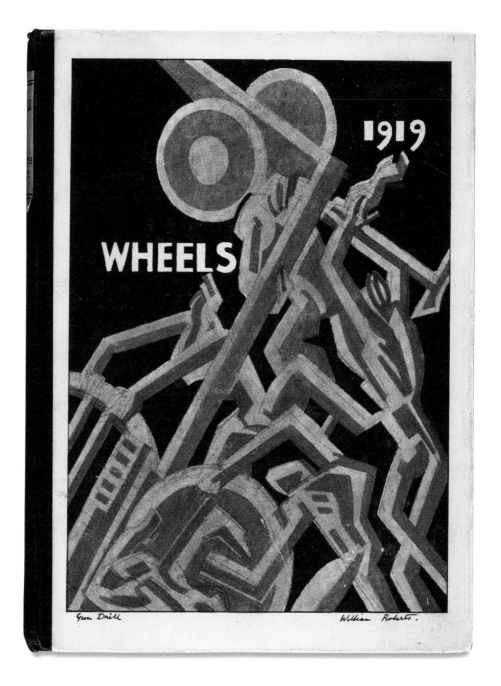

William Roberts, "Gun Drill," cover
illustration for *Wheels, 1919, Fourth
Cycle*, 1919, 7 ½ x 5 ½ in.,
B. H. Blackwell, Oxford, England

Wheels, a modernist poetry anthology edited
by Edith Sitwell, positioned itself in "open
revolt against conventional techniques and
subject but also against the war." The 1919 issue
featured a cover and endpapers designed
by William Roberts, a British artist associated
with the Vorticist movement who served
as a gunner in World War I.

But there was no silence; all the time the motor
omnibuses were turning their wheels and
changing their gear; like a vast nest
of Chinese boxes all of wrought
steel turning ceaselessly one
within another the city
murmured; on the top
of which the voices
cried aloud and
the petals of
myriads
of
flowers
flashed their
colours into the air.

—Virginia Woolf,
Kew Gardens, 1919

Whereas the war ripped apart the existing
world order, such nineteenth-century inventions as the
railroad, telegraph, steamship, and telephone continued
to bring humans closer together. By 1919, the automobile
and the airplane promised to radically alter the patterns
of everyday life yet again.

The number of registered cars in Los Angeles
County rose to 109,435, such that *Touring Topics,* the
Automobile Club of Southern California's magazine,
called for the development of a brake light, though the
term did not yet exist. Even in the early days of automobiles, ownership rates in California were among the
highest in the country. Road maps with brightly colored
networks could be deceptive. Particularly in the West,
maps did not distinguish between paved and unpaved
roads. Most traffic remained local, not long-haul, because

May 31, 1919—
A crew of aviators in
a U.S. Navy NC-4
aircraft complete
the world's first
transatlantic flight
after stopping in the
Azores to refuel.

June 15, 1919—
John "Jack" Alcock
and Arthur Brown
pilot the first non-
stop transatlantic
flight; they crash-
land in Ireland but
are unharmed.

Underwood & Underwood, *The Gondola
of the R.34, Britain's Largest Airship*,
1919, gelatin silver print, 7 ⅝ x 10 ⅛ in.

A newswire caption on the back of this
photograph indicates the airship's
glass observation car at right, the
enormous propeller, and its 670-foot
length. The airship remained aloft for
more than four hours during its initial
flight at Clydeside, Scotland.

the infrastructure was not there. Even so, adventuresome souls heard the call of the open road. Miss Claire Boltwood of Brooklyn, New York—the protagonist in Sinclair Lewis's novel *Free Air*—heads with her banker father to the Pacific Northwest in a Gomez-Dep roadster, finding liberation and love along the way.

A young Dwight D. Eisenhower learned firsthand the rigors of automobile travel. He left Washington, D.C., on July 7 in a convoy of eighty military vehicles. Because of poor road conditions, he arrived in San Francisco sixty-two days later.

The war propelled aviation technology forward (and upward). The first nonstop transatlantic flight repurposed a Vickers Vimy bomber developed by the Royal Air Force to carry John "Jack" Alcock, Arthur Brown, and a full tank of fuel from Newfoundland to Ireland. They crossed in sixteen hours, crash-landing, unharmed, on June 15, 1919. The war effort also improved lighter-than-air aircraft. German zeppelin bombing raids on British cities had breached the island fortress, terrifying citizens and galvanizing technological innovation. Shown here is the gondola of the British-made R.34 rigid airship that left the United Kingdom on July 2, 1919, and landed at Mineola, Long Island, on July 6, the first transatlantic crossing of this type of air vessel.

Mercury Aviation opened in Los Angeles, advertising short pleasure flights for the brave and long-haul trips to Bakersfield and Fresno. Flying remained an entertaining novelty, like an amusement park ride.

These aeronautical feats stirred the popular imagination. One author hoped airplanes could bring about "a modern Utopia on this earth" by the "commingling of nations"—a particularly quixotic view, given their destructive role in the war. Pilot guidebooks, like *The Way to Fly*, gave instructions on landing in crosswinds and engine maintenance. Books like *My Spiritual Aeroplane*, a Christian Science tract, used the airplane and pilot as metaphors for religious awakening.

September 6, 1919— The U.S. Army's first transcontinental motor convoy reaches San Francisco after leaving Washington, D.C., on July 7.

November 9, 1919— Felix the Cat appears in a Paramount Pictures cartoon short, *Feline Follies*.

November 19, 1919— Éamon de Valera, president of the Irish Republic, visits Los Angeles to gain support for independence from Great Britain.

Sinclair Lewis, *Free Air*, 1919, Harcourt, Brace, and Howe, New York; "Avion," *The Way to Fly*, 1919, C. A. Pearson, London; Arthur W. Judge, *Handbook of Modern Aeronautics*, 1919, Library Press, London

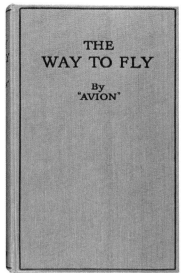

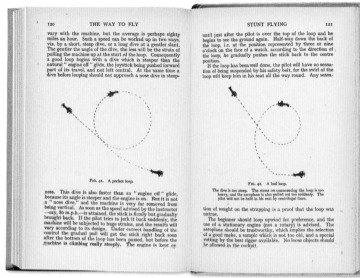

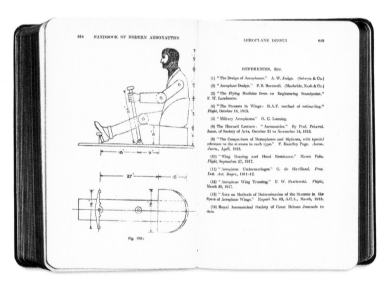

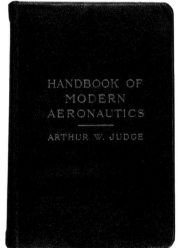

ABOVE
"A Perfect Loop" and "A Bad Loop,"
in *The Way to Fly*

BELOW
"The Appropriate Dimensions of
a Pilot in Position," in *Handbook
of Modern Aeronautics*

481237268470245680913026424752402619746163481

"French Chaser Aeroplane Flying over City 'Somewhere in France,'" in Charles B. Hayward, *Practical Aviation*, 1919, American Technical Society, Chicago

On the ground, Los Angeles County boomed, jumping from a population of 170,298 in 1900 to 936,455 in 1920, a more than fourfold increase. Southern California's growth rested on a fabric of steel rails for streetcars, copper wire for electrical signals, pipes for water, and smooth pavement for cars. Henry Huntington understood that with these overlaid networks, property would become ripe for development, and he profited by selling off subdivided lots along his streetcar lines. There is no movement without network.

And what of artistic movements, the isms sprinkled across the early twentieth century? Cubism, Suprematism, Imagism, Futurism, and Dadaism sloughed off tradition. Depicting the whirling nature of modern life, artists and writers gravitated to fragmented imagery and suggestions of movement to capture the disjunctive experience of the city. American artist Abraham Walkowitz portrayed the turbulent flow of traffic between skyscrapers (p. 150). For *L'Ode à Picasso*, French poet and filmmaker Jean Cocteau cut sentences into bits and used white space— measuring time by counting silences. In David Bomberg's *Russian Ballet*, stridently colored abstractions with angles, triangles, and bold diagonals allude to intertwined bodies and dancers dashing across a stage (pp. 156–57). Virginia Woolf's *Kew Gardens* is similarly kinesthetic (pp. 143, 154–55). Woolf layers road noise, human voices, and brightly colored flowers, each a note in a chord: engine, shout, petal. Voices of park-goers combine with flecks of colored flower petals and the roar of throttling buses to re-create the darting consciousness of a city dweller in a bustling London park.

ABOVE AND FACING
Jean Cocteau, *L'Ode à Picasso*, 1919,
François Bernouard, Paris

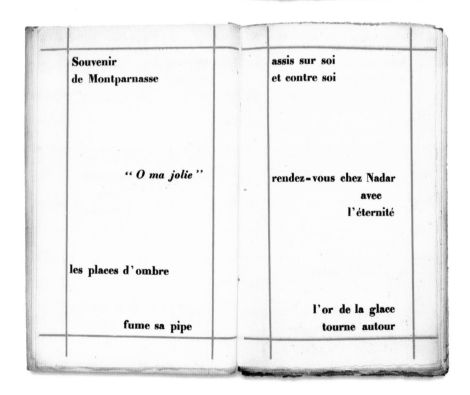

le rideau
de guignol

guillotine

Melpomène
et
Thalie

entre les deux tiges
du cadre

les tambours cobalt
couvrent leurs explications

bavardes

Souvenir
de Montparnasse

assis sur soi
et contre soi

" O ma jolie "

rendez-vous chez Nadar
avec
l'éternité

les places d'ombre

fume sa pipe

l'or de la glace
tourne autour

Modern City

American cities were full of railroad yards, skyscrapers, and streets teeming with traffic and
people. Joseph Pennell (1857–1926) depicts
the billowing steam of locomotives in St. Louis,
Missouri, a hub for transcontinental rail traffic.
Abraham Walkowitz (1880–1965) dabs the page
with ink to portray the city's energy. As opposed to
emphasizing movement, Earl Horter (1881–1940)
uses the glow from street level at nighttime to turn
tall buildings, including the spire of New York's
Fifth Avenue Presbyterian Church, into upwardly
lit entities that hint at mystery. *Dance at the
League* by Peggy Bacon (1895–1987) shows artists
in costume frenetically dancing. In the city, even
leisure is hurried.

ABOVE
Abraham Walkowitz, *New York
Skyscrapers*, 1919, brush and
black ink and wash on cream wove
paper, 19 x 12 ¾ in. Purchased
with funds from Ida Crotty for
Prints and Graphics

LEFT
Earl Horter, *The Dark Tower*, 1919,
etching, 6 ½ x 5 ¼ in., in *Twelve
Prints by Contemporary American
Artists*, 1919, E. Weyhe, New York

FOLLOWING SPREAD
Peggy Bacon, *Dance at the League*,
1919, drypoint, 9 ¼ x 11 ⅝ in.
Gift of Hannah S. Kully

Joseph Pennell, *Train Yard, St. Louis*, 1919,
lithograph, 19 ¾ x 17 in. Gift of Mr. and
Mrs. Brad Mishler

Hogarth Press

The Hogarth Press started out as a do-it-yourself operation with a handpress in the home of Virginia and Leonard Woolf. Virginia (1882–1941) set the type, and Leonard (1880–1969), along with a friend, printed the sheets. In 1919, their press issued these two booklets: poems by T. S. Eliot and Virginia's short story *Kew Gardens*, which included two woodcut illustrations by her sister Vanessa Bell. Roger Fry and Duncan Grant painted the covers by hand. The jarring colors—aquamarine on siennas and umbers, cyan on dark brown and yellow—are typical of Bloomsbury Group artists, who drew inspiration from the nonrepresentational colors of Henri Matisse. Hogarth Press went on to publish the English edition of Sigmund Freud's writings, novels by Christopher Isherwood, and works about Leo Tolstoy.

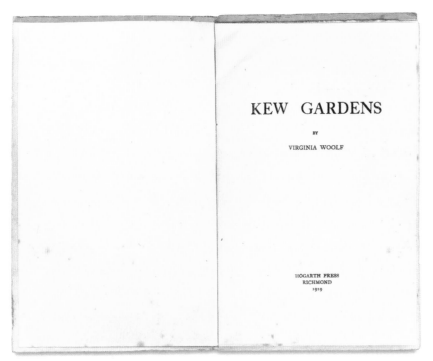

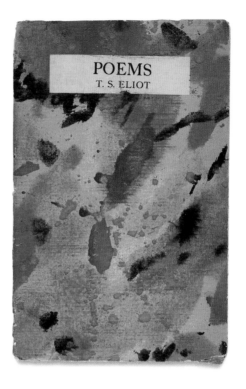

LEFT AND BOTTOM
Virginia Woolf, *Kew Gardens*, 1919,
Hogarth Press, Richmond, England

RIGHT
T. S. Eliot, *Poems*, 1919,
Hogarth Press, Richmond, England

LEFT AND FACING
David Bomberg, *Russian Ballet*,
1919, colored lithographs,
8 ⅝ x 5 ½ in. Purchased with funds
from the Huntington Gallery
Art Acquisition Fund

FOLLOWING SPREAD
George W. Haley, *President Woodrow
Wilson and Edith Wilson
on Santa Fe Street, Los Angeles*,
September 20, 1919, glass plate
negative, 4 x 5 in.

Impressions crowding collide

In the summer of 1919, the British artist David
Bomberg (1890–1957) attended a performance by
the Ballets Russes of *La Boutique Fantasque* (The
Magic Toy Shop), a ballet with music by Ottorino
Respighi. Staged at London's Alhambra Theatre,
with sets and costumes by French painter
André Derain, the piece told of toys come to life
and misbehaving. Impressed by the spectacle,
Bomberg printed this book of bold lithographs
and juxtaposed them with sentence fragments.
These putative poetic captions do not explain the
images; rather, they amplify their disorienting
effect. Indeed, the lithographs vibrate with energy,
acting as metaphors for the dizzying experience
of modern, postwar life. Bomberg was a Vorticist,
part of a London-based avant-garde movement
that, in 1914, attacked representational art and
took up the cause of abstraction. His lithographs
demonstrate a return to this prewar fascination
with radical abstraction and its potential for
dislocation and sensory overload.

On the following spread, President
Woodrow Wilson and First Lady
Edith Wilson head to Los Angeles's
Shrine Auditorium for the president's rousing speech promoting the
League of Nations plan. The couple
would encounter photographers and
shrieking crowds along the ten-mile
route through downtown. The press
later reported that 50,000 people were
turned away at the auditorium doors.

Methodic discord startles . . . .

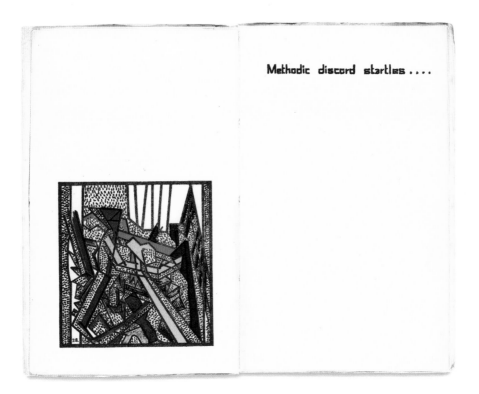

Impressions crowding collide
with movement round us —

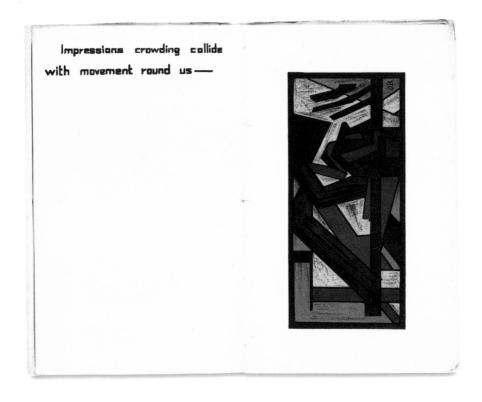

The great copper mine of the "Consolidated" at Ruth, Nev.

A few of the six thousand cattle on Alpine Ranch

In the desert, dead animals just dry up

East of Reno the highway is on an abandoned railroad grade

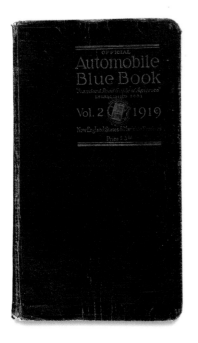

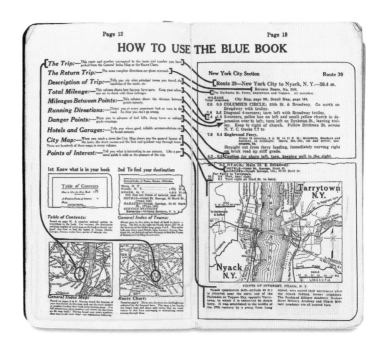

ABOVE
(left and right) *Official Automobile
Blue Book*, vol. 2, *New England
States and Maritime Provinces*, 1919,
Automobile Blue Book Publishing,
New York

FACING
Sidney D. Waldon, *Sage Brush and
Sequoia*, 1919, privately published
in edition of twelve copies, letterpress
and gelatin silver photographs

FOLLOWING SPREAD
Pacific Electric Railway Company,
*Map of Pacific Electric Railway System
in Southern California*, 1912–19, ink on
blueline print (reprographic copy),
30 x 53 in.

On the Road

A group of businessmen friends pledged to see America
at the end of World War I. On July 8, 1919, the twelve
men—including famed aviator Orville Wright—left
Denver bound for California, driving a Packard and
three Cadillacs. They loaded the luxury automobiles,
each named after a Native American group, with
high-end accessories: goose-down sleeping bags,
air mattresses, three cameras, and sixty rolls of
film. They also brought the *Official Automobile Blue
Book*, an indispensable touring guide. After the
seventeen-day journey, they created a deluxe album
of photographs and text memorializing the trip.
The trek, mostly over rugged and unpaved terrain,
celebrated a national peace as well as a postwar
healing, a fraternal bond "consecrated amid the
vastness and great silences of the West."

MAP OF
PACIFIC ELECTRIC RAILWAY SYSTEM
IN
SOUTHERN CALIFORNIA

JULY 1912
REVISED APRIL 1918

REVISED TO:-
OCT. 14, 1918.
JUNE 23, 1919.
NOV. 24, 1919.

SCALE IN FEET PER INCH
SCALE IN MILES

Statement 1

"TUESDAY"

Form 105A—1M-10-18
Com. Lib. Led.
19x24-36 Order 9691

LOS ANGELES RAILWAY
DAILY CASH STATEMENT

Condition of weather Cloudy   May 27th 1919
Attraction Base Ball — Prize Fight

Balance Previous Day			103 874 51
RECEIPTS				
Agents and Conductors	20 360 65		
School Tickets	240 00		
Regular Tickets			
U. S. Gov. Tickets			
Special Cars	25 00		
Pay Roll Deductions	2 205 50		
Misc'l. Small Bills, Etc.	79 65		
3rd Liberty Bonds	356 25		
4th Liberty Bonds	353 75		
5th " "	823 75	24 444 55
DISBURSEMENTS			128 319 06
Pay Roll Vouchers	23 095 15		
Audited Vouchers	4 756 28	27 851 43
#46403			
Balance This Date			100 467 63
VERIFICATION			
Bank Balance	57 665 42		
Currency and Checks	42 802 21	100 467 63
Previous Year			
Condition of Weather	Cloudy & Rain		
Attraction	Baseball — Prize Fight		
Conductor's Collection this day this year	20 360 65		
Conductor's Collection this day last year	16 871 25		
Average Daily for month this year	20 252 47		
Average Daily for month last year	17 911 25		
Total Month to date this year	546 816 60		
Total Month to date last year	483 603 85		
Total Month to date year before last	415 673 70		

Auditor

Statement 2

"Saturday"

Form 105A—1M 4-19
Com. Lib. Led.
19x24-36 Order 9804

LOS ANGELES RAILWAY
DAILY CASH STATEMENT

Condition of Weather September 20th 1919
Attraction President Wilson - Strike

Balance Previous Day		123 382 91
RECEIPTS			
Agents and Conductors	21 445 15	
School Tickets	125 00	
Regular Tickets		
U. S. Gov. Tickets		
Special Cars		
Pay Roll Deductions		
Misc'l. Small Bills, Etc.	137 83	
3rd Liberty Bonds	17 50	
4th Liberty Bonds	43 75	
V. Lib. Bond	110 00	
P. E. Ry. Co.	4 192 44	
L. A. Gas, & Elec	288 33	
Western Elec.	68 48	26 428 48
DISBURSEMENTS		149 811 39
Pay Roll Vouchers		
Audited Vouchers	6 296 11	
So. Cal. Ed. Co	50 842 20	57 138 31
Balance This Date		92 673 08
VERIFICATION		
Bank Balance	50 536 06	
Currency and Checks	42 137 02	92 673 08
Previous Year		
Condition of Weather	Clear	
Attraction	Heroes Day Exposition Park	
Conductor's Collection this day this year	21 445 15	
Conductor's Collection this day last year	21 159 75	
Average Daily for month this year	17 434 87	
Average Daily for month last year	18 167 90	
Total Month to date this year	348 597 50	
Total Month to date last year	363 356 00	
Total Month to date year before last	343 511 35	

Auditor

Statement 3

Form 105A—1M 4-19
Com. Lib. Led.
19x24-36 Order 9804

LOS ANGELES RAILWAY
DAILY CASH STATEMENT

Condition of Weather November 11th 1919
Attraction Armistice Day

Balance Previous Day		117 668 59
RECEIPTS			
Agents and Conductors	18 817 90	
School Tickets	266 00	
Regular Tickets		
U. S. Gov. Tickets		
Special Cars		
Pay Roll Deductions	1 522 50	
Misc'l. Small Bills, Etc.	109 86	20 716 26
3rd Liberty Bonds		
4th Liberty Bonds		
DISBURSEMENTS		138 384 85
Pay Roll Vouchers		
Audited Vouchers		
#48692		
Balance This Date		138 384 85
VERIFICATION		
Bank Balance	70 497 37	
Currency and Checks	67 887 48	138 384 85
Previous Year		
Condition of Weather	Cloudy	
Attraction	None	
Conductor's Collection this day this year	18 817 90	
Conductor's Collection this day last year	16 396 95	
Average Daily for month this year	20 272 99	
Average Daily for month last year	15 039 09	
Total Month to date this year	223002 85	
Total Month to date last year	165 430 05	
Total Month to date year before last	191 939 50	

Auditor

Mass Transit

Henry Huntington created a regional transportation system stretching a thousand steel miles from "the mountains to the sea." Red and yellow streetcars, jaunty symbols of the Pacific Electric and Los Angeles Railway, spun out from city center hundreds of miles in every direction to the fledgling suburbs Huntington owned. Whereas the Pacific Electric took people to the periphery of the metropolis—to Riverside, San Bernardino, and down the Orange County coast—the Los Angeles Railway, a central hub, ferried commuters to downtown from nearby neighborhoods. The company kept daily cash statements recording weather conditions and special events to account for ridership ebbs and flows. For instance, on a clear Saturday, September 20, 1919, President Wilson promoted his League of Nations peace proposal to cheering, boisterous crowds in Exposition Park. Conductors collected almost $21,500 in fares that day. A month prior, railway officials claimed to be operating at a loss when employees staged an unsuccessful strike.

"TUESDAY"

Form 105A—1M 4-19
Com. Lia. Led.
19x24-36 Order 9804

LOS ANGELES RAILWAY
DAILY CASH STATEMENT

Condition of Weather November 18th 19 19
Attraction Prize Fight

Balance Previous Day			150	164 39
RECEIPTS				
Agents and Conductors	21	738 50		
School Tickets		286 00		
Regular Tickets				
U. S. Gov. Tickets				
Special Cars				
Pay Roll Deductions				
Misc'l. Small Bills, Etc.		123 25		
3rd Liberty Bonds				
4th Liberty Bonds		20 00		
V. Lib. Bond		41 25		
Coop. Assoc.		259 17		
			22	468 17
DISBURSEMENTS			172	632 56
Pay Roll Vouchers				
Audited Vouchers			2	054 20
#48791				
Balance This Date			170	578 36
VERIFICATION				
Bank Balance	134	614 31		
Currency and Checks	35	964 05	170	578 36
Previous Year				
Condition of Weather Rain				
Attraction None				
Conductor's Collection this day this year			21	738 50
Conductor's Collection this day last year			15	846 05
Average Daily for month this year			20	661 03
Average Daily for month last year			15	111 31
Total Month to date this year			371	898 55
Total Month to date last year			272	006 55
Total Month to date year before last			317	330 50

Auditor

"THURSDAY"

Form 105A—1M 4-19
Com. Lia. Led.
19x24-36 Order 9804

LOS ANGELES RAILWAY
DAILY CASH STATEMENT

Condition of Weather November 20th 19 19
Attraction De Valera Parade

Balance Previous Day			126	622 07
RECEIPTS				
Agents and Conductors	21	644 85		
School Tickets		226 00		
Regular Tickets				
U. S. Gov. Tickets				
Special Cars				
Pay Roll Deductions				
Misc'l. Small Bills, Etc.		242 30		
3rd Liberty Bonds				
4th Liberty Bonds		50 00		
V. Lib. Bond		32 50		
			22	195 65
DISBURSEMENTS			148	817 72
Pay Roll Vouchers				
Audited Vouchers			21	555 28
#48825				
Balance This Date			127	262 44
VERIFICATION				
Bank Balance	91	311 82		
Currency and Checks	35	950 62	127	262 44
Previous Year				
Condition of Weather Clear				
Attraction None				
Conductor's Collection this day this year			21	644 85
Conductor's Collection this day last year			16	406 45
Average Daily for month this year			20	763 27
Average Daily for month last year			15	232 93
Total Month to date this year			415	265 35
Total Month to date last year			304	658 55
Total Month to date year before last			253	568 95

Auditor

"MONDAY"

Form 105A—1M 4-19
Com. Lia. Led.
19x24-36 Order 9804

LOS ANGELES RAILWAY
DAILY CASH STATEMENT

Condition of Weather December 1st 19 19
Attraction None

Balance Previous Day			76	703 67
RECEIPTS				
Agents and Conductors	22	661 40		
School Tickets		32 00		
Regular Tickets				
U. S. Gov. Tickets				
Special Cars				
Pay Roll Deductions				
Misc'l. Small Bills, Etc.		198 17		
3rd Liberty Bonds				
4th Liberty Bonds		30 00		
V. Lib. Bond		142 50		
Mrs. E. A. Bryant		64 65		
Times Mirror Co.		74 48		
H. L. & Imp. Co.		140 78		
			23	343 98
DISBURSEMENTS			100	047 65
Pay Roll Vouchers				
Audited Vouchers		777 04		
L. A. Trust &Sav.	50	000 00		
			50	777 04
Balance This Date			49	270 61
VERIFICATION				
Bank Balance	13	096 14		
Currency and Checks	36	174 47	49	270 61
Previous Year				
Condition of Weather Clear				
Attraction Influenza Ban lifted				
Conductor's Collection this day this year			22	661 40
Conductor's Collection this day last year			19	419 00
Average Daily for month this year			22	661 40
Average Daily for month last year			10	833 35
Total Month to date this year			22	661 40
Total Month to date last year			10	833 35
Total Month to date year before last			19	698 05

Auditor

ABOVE
Los Angeles Railway daily cash statements, May, September, November, and December 1919

FOLLOWING SPREADS
(pages 166–67) *Pacific Electric Streetcar Tracks Looking North on Fair Oaks Avenue, Pasadena, California*, ca. 1919, film positive, 3 ¾ x 4 ¾ in.
(pages 168–69) Pacific Electric Railway Company, *Passengers on Pacific Electric's Old Mission-Balloon Route Trolley Trip*, ca. 1919, gelatin silver print, 5 x 7 in.

Lighting the Way

On a celebratory October evening at a Los Angeles hotel, a young woman attired as Mercury stood atop a banquet table before a group of Southern California Edison executives. Under a dazzling display of lights, she presented a congratulatory telegram acknowledging the region as a leader in world electrification. And why not? The Edison corporation had recently opened a gleaming headquarters with state-of-the art products and glowing appliances on display. A workforce over two thousand strong provided light and power to more than a million Southern Californians spread out across 55,000 square miles. The future had arrived, and it was electric.

G. Haven Bishop, *Display in Southern California Edison's 4th Street Offices of the New Edison Mazda Electric Light Bulbs*, 1919, glass plate negative, 10 15/16 x 9 3/16 in.

Henry Huntington

Henry Huntington's contemporaries described him as a builder above all else.

Build he did. Huntington constructed a railroad career and a Southern California dynasty in transportation and real estate. He amassed millions through financial canniness and inheritance. He fashioned a second marriage he considered a success. He assembled a world-renowned collection of books, art, and plants at a 600-acre Eden he called "the ranch."

Huntington's desire to build an institution grew over time. He had watched Collis and Arabella spend hundreds of thousands funding charitable causes. Archer, Arabella's bookish son, founded the Hispanic Society of America in 1904 as a research library and art museum devoted to the history, art, and culture of Spain. Archer encouraged Huntington to specialize in his collecting, too. "I sing but one song [to H. E.]," he confided in his diary, "keep to English."

Archer also shared the Hispanic Society's founding documents, its governing structure, its principles and ideals. He made a rough drawing of a library at Huntington's request. The eventual building was modeled on Archer's sketch: three substantial wings that formed a sideways "E."

The charismatic astronomer George Ellery Hale proselytized Huntington for over a decade as well. Hale wanted to make Southern California a global center for science, humanities, and the arts. Huntington's collections were key to this cultural scheme.

Huntington kept his own counsel. Then, what had been private, went public. In September 1919, the press heralded the debut of a Southern California institution, the first of its kind. The Henry E. Huntington Library and Art Gallery was to be a "free public library, art gallery, museum and park" dedicated to the advancement of learning in the arts and sciences.

The announcement signaled the realization of Huntington's great dream: building a lasting monument to all he had achieved, inscribed with his name.

Arabella Huntington

Arabella constructed a persona with exacting care.

After becoming Mrs. Collis P. Huntington in 1884, she set about fashioning a self commensurate with her elevated station in society. She read Russian history each morning from seven until eight, followed by a thirty-minute singing lesson to cultivate her voice. Private tutors came weekly to her New York palace, drilling her hour after hour in Spanish and French.

She gained a reputation as a freewheeling spender, albeit one with a discerning eye. Belle both charmed and intimidated dealers as they obsequiously peddled their wares. "Mrs. Huntington allows herself manners which even the Empress of Germany cannot afford!" a spurned merchant huffed.

Belle appeared cool and reserved in public and to people she did not trust. She revealed a softer, more approachable side to children and animals of all kinds. She wrote affectionate, teasing letters to family, and indulged friends with money and gifts. In the latter half of her life, she worked hard to conceal that she was almost fully deaf and blind. Few could penetrate the fortress Belle built around herself.

What beat at the heart of Belle's agenda? In a letter to Archer, her pampered, urbane son, she hinted at one source of her formal bearing and unrelenting drive: "It is the duty of each to display himself as something important," she wrote.

Archer pondered that statement. "I hope not," he replied.

One of the largest and most
extensive private libraries in
the world is being built at
San Marino...and when
this is completed it also
will be conveyed
to the public.

—"$2,500,000 Gift of Art Objects to
Los Angeles," *Chicago Tribune*,
September 15, 1919

That Southern California needs an
institution of higher education
which gives a degree from
the State is evident.

—"A Real College: Proposed Merging of Los Angeles
State Normal School with University of California,"
Los Angeles Times, January 23, 1919

The new symphony is to be known as
the Los Angeles Philharmonic Orchestra. A fund of $100,000 has
been raised and additional
money is to be provided to
cover any deficit that
may be incurred.

—"New Orchestra is Organized,"
Los Angeles Times, June 11, 1919

FACING
William F. Hertrich, *Construction
of the Library Building, Looking
Southeast, Showing the West Side of
the West Wing* (detail), December 19,
1919, gelatin silver print, 4 ¼ x 6 ⅜ in.

INSERT
(front) Arnold Genthe, *Henry E.
Huntington in the Library of His
New York Residence* (detail), ca. 1917,
gelatin silver print, 9 ¾ x 6 ⅞ in.;
(back) *Arabella Huntington* (detail),
ca. 1903. Courtesy of The Hispanic
Society of America, New York

William F. Hertrich, *Construction of the Library Building*,
December 20, 1919 (top), and December 14, 1919 (bottom),
gelatin silver prints, 4 ¼ x 6 ⅜ in. each

182

Knowing that all roads led to another world war, one cannot look back on 1919 without foreboding. The Great War's targeting of civilian populations with blockades, bombings, forced relocations, and the Armenian Genocide would find ghastly parallels in World War II.

From the vantage point of 1919, however, the fighting was over and optimism reigned. H. G. Wells called it "the war that will end war," a final push to solve an age-old human problem. French historians Stéphane Audoin-Rouzeau and Annette Becker observe that, during the conflict, both sides "believed they were waging the war because it would bring a new radiant world in the future."

Huntington sat for a conversation with the *Los Angeles Times* and shared this spirit of positivity. In the interview, he first pointed out the problems with the federal government's takeover of railroads, the high cost of living brought on by inflation (upwards of 60 percent over a five-year period), and labor agitation. "The unrest in Europe is felt here," he said. "The I.W.W. movement here is of the same brand as Russian Bolshevism." While aware of strife, he was bullish on America's future: "I feel confident that an era of good business is at hand." He believed in the League of Nations, so long as it respected the Monroe Doctrine and let the United States keep Latin America as a sphere of influence and control.

Huntington's confidence reverberated in his personal affairs that year. On January 12, 1919, the *Los Angeles Times* announced that plans were underway for construction of a library building to house Huntington's world-famous collection. His library staff started the immense task of relocating the library from New York City to San Marino. By then, two of the three collecting areas at The Huntington were already in place. Under the watchful eye of William Hertrich, the palm, desert, rose, and Japanese gardens were planted. The mansion, designed by Myron Hunt, was completed in 1910 and filled with Huntington's paintings, tapestries, and sculptures.

February 5, 1919— Charlie Chaplin, Douglas Fairbanks, Mary Pickford, and D. W. Griffith launch motion picture studio United Artists.

February 20, 1919— Premiere of Oscar Micheaux's *The Homesteader*, the first feature-length film produced by an African American for an African-American audience.

March 1919— Huntington's library catalogers are absent a total of 408 hours from January through March due to the influenza pandemic.

April 12, 1919— Walter Gropius founds the Bauhaus art school in Weimar, Germany.

Book of Hours, use of Rome, early sixteenth century, France; John Ruskin, *The Seven Lamps of Architecture*, 1849; Benjamin Franklin, *Autobiography*, autograph manuscript, 1771–89

July 28, 1919—
International Astronomical Union is formed in Brussels, Belgium.

September 18, 1919—
First meeting of The Huntington Library's Board of Trustees: Howard E. Huntington, William E. Dunn, George S. Patton, and George Ellery Hale attend.

October 29, 1919—
International Labor Organization is established to promote fair and humane labor standards in participating League of Nations countries.

With the construction of the library building, the keystone fell into place for the tripartite division of The Huntington today.

Henry Huntington continued to buy aggressively. He placed successful bids at fifty rare book and manuscript auctions in 1919, amplifying his holdings with superlative purchases from distinguished libraries like Herschel V. Jones, Britwell Court, Frederic Halsey, and many others. In August, before the Huntingtons signed the indenture, dealer A. S. W. Rosenbach hand delivered $121,000 worth of sixteenth- and early seventeenth-century Shakespearean works to the house.

Others in the region shared Huntington's sunny outlook. The California legislature founded UCLA as the Southern Branch of the University of California, and William Andrews Clark Jr. started the Los Angeles Philharmonic. Griffith J. Griffith bequeathed money to construct the Greek Theatre in his namesake park.

In 1919, Huntington founded an institution, settled on his burial site, paid record prices for books, and, curiously, purchased four portraits of George Washington (pp. 219–21). Why so many? Yes, there was an increased demand from collectors that year, as the author of the article "Growth of Interest in Washington Portraits" observed in the *American Magazine of Art*. Perhaps he followed a trend. But could it be that he saw a fellow builder and founder? Could it be that Washington's voluntary retreat from public life and relinquishing of power after two terms as president provided a model for Huntington to emulate? The paradox of a person's legacy is that it rests with others. Huntington's indenture empowered five trustees—friends and family in whom he had placed great faith—and amounted to an admission that his library would go on without him.

184

Myron Hunt, *The Henry Huntington Library*,
presentation drawing, ca. 1919,
ink on linen, 34 ⅜ x 25 ⅜ in.

Cut and Dried

These specimens are from plants that were likely on Huntington's property in 1919. The *Phytolacca dioica*, commonly known as ombú, came from a seed received in 1912 from the botanical garden in Buenos Aires, Argentina. That same ombú is still found in the Jungle Garden. *Laurus nobilis*, or bay laurel, is native to the Mediterranean and thrives in the dry California climate. The cutting probably came from a hedge of bay trees that encircle the flagpole, which arrived in 1909. Botanists Bonnie C. Templeton and Eric Walther made the first attempt to systematically inventory the enormous plant collection, beginning in 1931. They clipped hundreds of vouchers, or samples, noting date of collection, genus and species, and native origin. Housed in the institution's herbarium, the 15,000 preserved specimens are mounted on paper sheets for study, comparison, and identification.

ABOVE
(top) *Phytolacca dioica* and (bottom) *Laurus nobilis*, 1931, 16 ½ x 11 ½ in. each, herbarium specimens collected by Bonnie C. Templeton and Eric Walther

FACING
William F. Hertrich, *Neobuxbaumia euphorbioides (Cephalocereus euphorbioides)*, 1925, lantern slide, 4 x 3 ¼ in.

Build

William Hertrich supervised a desert garden expansion around 1925 that involved moving and transplanting cacti, aloes, agaves, and other plants, some weighing between two and five tons. He recorded the herculean effort with his camera, using these lantern slides to illustrate lectures and talks. By this time, the collection was "the largest [one] in the world of desert specimens planted out of doors."

W. Hertrich
1925

```
TRACT #2
        Boxes      Net      Average
Nav     1714     $584.16    .34081
Val      266      108.25    .40695
        1980     $692.41    .34970

TRACT #1
        Boxes      Net      Average
.Nav     635     $290.64    .4577

SHORB STATION
        Boxes      Net      Average
Nav     1905    $1027.29    .53925
```

```
CAGE #1
1  Trio golden Pheasant
1    "   silver   do
1    "   Lady Amherst Pheas.
1    "   Reeves Pheasant

5  Pair Hartz Mt. Canaries
4    "   Chinese linnets
1    "   European   do
3    "   Roller Canaries
3        Goldfinches
2    "   Paris trumpeters

CAGE #2
3  Mexican Blue Jays
1  Mountain   do
2  S. A. double bar Jays
2  European Blue Jays
1  Pair Brazil Glassy B.Jays
1  Pair Toucans
2  Cardinals
1  Mongolian Grass beak
1  Pair Aust. Magpie
1  Pair Laughin Jackass
```

Revolvers to main House

Miss Larsen   271 512
McGillivray   260 481

```
Percent of wage increases
San M. R. 1-1-18 to 10-1-18
Gio Mazzin          18.7%
Chas. Handforth     14.3
P. Fritzinger        5.5
Paul Kley            5.2
Otto Veit           10.8
C. Schneider        28.5
Chas. Akerman        8.
T. Gotto             7.7
John Gombotz         6.8
G. L. Brown          9.
Louis Wees          15.2
F. Nelson
C. E. Williams      10.
J. Muller
Paul Muller         20.
J. F. Morris        25.2
W. S. Cockrell
W. A. Boswell       25.2
P. Giovannoli       18.8
L. B. Scott         25.2
H. H. Welch          8.3
Geo. Chaplin        13.3
Gus Luttenberg      15.2
C. F. Moss           7.1
D. M. Manning       15.2

                    over.
```

Accounting

William Hertrich—chief designer of Huntington's ranch—carried a little three-ring notebook wherever he went. Penciled scribblings and typewritten lists record a jumble of calculations and reminders: average yields of oranges and avocados per tree; the types of birds (five hundred altogether) in each aviary cage; the percentage of salary increases for dozens of staff; the combination to a library vault; the serial numbers for two revolvers kept in the house; as well as detailed labor and material costs for all the grading, hauling, boxing, digging, draining, excavating, building, plowing, and pruning he superintended.

Squeezing the Orange

Huntington entertained a citrus scheme to
bankroll his ranch. William Hertrich, his superintendent, planted eighty-five experimental
acres of oranges in 1916, obsessively monitoring
growth rates, fertilizer formulas, and net profits
calculated both by tree and by crate. Labor was
carefully tracked, too. In 1919, workers with
Mexican surnames made between 3 and 4 dollars
per day. Those with European surnames made
up to 50 percent more. At the peak, 64,000 crates
of Huntington's Toucan Brand oranges made an
impressive $134,000 in all. Years of hard freezes
ultimately dashed Huntington's agricultural
hopes. The founder discarded his initial idea,
selling three hundred acres around 1926 to help
pay for his library and art gallery.

Time for Week ending Aug 30 19 19

NAMES	S	M	T	W	T	F	S	Total Time	Rate p. day	Total Amount	Amount Due Extra	Amount Paid	Rec'd Payment Total Boxes
Ramirez	9	3	x	~	-	-	-	12	33⅓	400	108	508	85
Ramirez	9	3	x	-	-	-	-	12	"	400	26 156	556	93
Juarez	5	-	x	-	-	-	-	5	"	167		167	30
Rodriguez	9	-	x	-	-	-	-	9	"	360	12 102	402	67
Aguirre	9	3	x	-	-	-	-	12	"	400	6	406	68
Romo	9	3	x	-	-	-	-	12	"	400	66	466	78
Cardona	9	3	x	-	-	-	-	12	"	400		400	63
L Reyes	9	3	x	-	-	-	-	12	"	400	8 48	448	78
L Casas	0	3	x	-	-	-	-	3	"	100		100	17
A Mercado	9	3	x	-	-	-	-	12	"	400	7 12	412	69
Castillo	9	3	x	-	-	-	-	12	"	400	14 114	514	86
Reyes	9	3	x	-	-	-	-	12	"	400	58 348	748	12 5
Acevedo	9	3	x	-	-	-	-	12	"	400	26 456	856	143
												999	
Acevedo	9	8				5	19	40	760		77 837	77	
Juarez body	4	3					7	36			252		
											7072		
anys													
H Salazar	9	6½					15½	75 00			1200		
A. Smith	9	5	x	9	x	5	28	7 00			2177		
											10449		
Oldham Truck							4	1 50	600				

Juarez 16⁷ 4/9
25/9
91

Insurance
ckies 70.72
wlis 14.33
91.05

Authors Club

On the evening of December 18, 1919, Henry Huntington entertained members of the prestigious New York Authors Club in the library of his Fifth Avenue home. He had voraciously acquired complete libraries, unique manuscripts, and rare books over twenty years, building one of the greatest private collections in the world. That night, he eagerly shared the Anglo-American treasures in which—according to his librarian—"he took especial pride" with a discerning audience of writers and connoisseurs. Huntington laid out a choice sampling of thirty-five items dating from the eleventh century through the nineteenth: one-of-a-kind handwritten documents by history's "great men," rare first editions, an elaborately illuminated religious tome, classics of English literature, Shakespeare's works, and American historical gems. The tantalizing selection offered the merest taste of the bibliographic cornucopia that the prodigious collector had assembled, providing the only insight into purchases that Huntington prized above all else. A few of the items showcased at that exclusive event are described on the pages that follow.

FACING
Second-Floor Library of Henry E. Huntington's Fifth Avenue Residence, New York (detail), 1915, gelatin silver print, 4 ½ x 5 ¾ in.

Gilded Prayers

Books of Hours such as this one were prayer books
that included Psalms, Bible passages, and interces-
sions, though content varied, depending on geography
and the patron's desires. In the fifteenth and early
sixteenth centuries, Books of Hours were the most
common type of publication, owned by a swath of
people, especially women, from the literate middle
class to royalty. The Book of Hours here was likely
commissioned by an extremely wealthy person, given
its exquisite quality and expensive materials,
including aquamarine pigment and gold. Depicted
on the facing page at top is the Annunciation, as
described in the Gospel according to Luke, in which
the Angel Gabriel tells the Virgin Mary that she
will give birth to Jesus, the Son of God. The dove
symbolizes her conception by the Holy Spirit, and
the white lilies on the opposite page signal her purity.
The Master of Claude, an unnamed illuminator who
worked for Queen Claude of France, probably painted
the figure of the Virgin Mary in her chamber, while
another unnamed artist focused on the butterflies
and flowers in the margins.

FACING
(top) "Annunciation," in *Book of Hours*,
use of Rome, early sixteenth century,
France, pigment on parchment,
page: 8 ¾ x 5 ½ in.; (bottom)
"Visitation," in *Book of Hours*, use of
Rome, early sixteenth century,
France, pigment on parchment, page:
8 ¾ x 5 ½ in. Purchased by Henry E.
Huntington, 1918

Ibi ergo propter parasceuen iudeorum
quia iuxta erat monumentum posuerunt
Iesum. Deo gratias. ¶ Oratio.

Eus qui manus tuas & pedes tu
os & totum corpus tuum pro no
bis peccatoribus in ligno crucis posuisti.
& coronam spineam a iudeis in despe
ctu tui sacratissimi nominis super caput
tuum impositam sustinuisti. & quinq3
vulnera pro nobis peccatoribus in ligno
crucis passus fuisti: da nobis hodie & q̃
tidie. vsum penitentie. & abstinentie. pa
tientie. humilitatis. castitatis. lume. sen
sum & intellectum & puram conscientiam
vsq3 in finem. Iesu christe saluator mun
di. Qui cum patre & spiritusancto viuis
& regnas deus.

Per.

Officium beatissime virginis Marie se
cundum vsum Romane
ecclesie. feliciter
inci
pit.

Omine labia mea aperies.
Et os meum annuncia
bit laudem tuam.
Deus in adiutoriū meū intende

tu ad liberandum suscepturus homi
nem, non horruisti virginis vterum.
Tu deuicto mortis aculeo: aperuisti cre
dentibus regna celorum.
Tu ad dexteram dei sedes in glõria pris
Iudex crederis esse venturus.
Te ergo quesumus famulis tuis sub
ueni: quos precioso sanguine redemisti.
Æterna fac cum sanctis tuis: in gloria
numerari. Saluum fac populum tu
um domine. & benedic hereditati tue.
Et rege eos. & extolle illos vsq3 in eter
nū. Per singulos dies bndicim9 te. num.
Et laudamus nomen tuum in secu
lum. & in seculum seculi.
Dignare domine die isto: sine pec
cato nos custodire.
Miserere nostri dñe. miserere nostri.
Fiat misericordia tua domine super
nos: quemadmodū sperauimus in te.
In te domine speraui: non confun
dar ineternum.

¶ Ad laudes.

Eus in adiutorium meum
intende.
Domine ad adiuuādum.
Gloria patri. Sicut erat. á Assūpta. ps
Ominus regnauit decorem in
dutus est: indutus est domin9
fortitudinem & precinxit se.

Wôpanâôt8âôk

English missionary John Eliot (1604–1690) supervised
the publication of a phonetic translation of the Bible
in Wôpanâôt8âôk, the language of the Wôpanâak people
living in Massachusetts. The names of some of
the native speakers who worked on the translation are
known today, including Job Nesuton, John Sassamon,
Caleb Cheeshahtyâmuk, and Joel Hiacoombs. The
Wampanoag Bible was the first in a Native American
language and the first Bible printed in North America.
To underwrite the expense of this complex project,
the Society for the Propagation of the Gospel in
New England, founded in 1649, sought donations in
England. For Puritans, direct access to God's Word was
required for true conversion. Prior to the 1670s, they
encouraged indigenous people to worship and sing
Psalms in their own languages. Though the Wôpanâak
people's language became extinct in the nineteenth
century, jessie 'little doe' baird, an MIT-trained ling-
uist, leads an effort to revive it and has established
the Wôpanâak Language Reclamation Project.

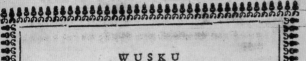

WUSKU
WUTTESTAMENTUM
NUL-LORDUMUN
JESUS CHRIST
Nuppoquohwuſſuaeneûmun.

CAMBRIDGE:

Printed by *Samuel Green* and *Marmaduke Johnson.*
MDCLXI.

Redcoat's Journal

Colonel John André (1750–1780), who served with the British forces during the Revolutionary War, is best known for his role as chief intermediary for Benedict Arnold, an American army officer, in the foiled plot to surrender West Point to the British. Whereas the traitor Arnold escaped and received a commission as brigadier general in the British army, André was hanged as a spy. The maps reproduced here are from André's journal, kept from June 11, 1777, to November 15, 1778. They depict battles like Brandywine as well as such strategic areas as the fortresses of Mud Island on the Delaware River near Philadelphia. André's skills as a draftsman are on display in these beautiful, delicately rendered maps, which he most likely prepared for his commanding officer.

2.

Battle of Brandewyne
on the 11th September 1777 —

This plan is intended to show chiefly
the operations on the left, by tracing the
general Course each Corps took.
The Yellow parts are the places near
which the Rebels made most opposition

The 33d Reg.t was halted for a little
while in front of the Village of Dilworth
but joined the Brigade soon after. —

Part of the 42.d and the
15.th Regiment were
drawn up first on the
hill A afterwards on
B to cover the Baggage

Birmingham Meeting

Dilworth Village.

Head Quar.

3.d Brig.e

Rebel Battery of two guns

Chad's Ford where Gen.l Knyphausen passed.

Road to Concord, Chester & Phila.delphia

Place where 3000 of the Rebels resolved to attack part of Gen.l Knyphausen's Corps

HM 3087

Mud Island
with the Operations for
reducing it.—

15th Nov.r 1777

Ferry House.

Mr Whipps's

Philadelphia

The River

The Pest House

2. Med.r 12 p.

Province Island.

2. 32 poun.r
a med.r 12. p.

Low marshy Grounds.—

an 18 pounder.

Mingo Creek

Profile of the
Fort

A Dyke

Carpenters

Island

Elevation

Profile

Very low ground
which was overflowed
from the Rebels having
the Dykes.—

Little Mud Island

A 32 p.r from the floating Batt.y

A Dyke

A Floating Battery with 2. 32 p.rs
was moored hereabouts
on the 14th Nov.r but towed off
again in the night.—

Delaware River

MUD I.

6. 24 pounders

an 8 Inch Mortar

an 8 Inch Howitzer

Wharf

an 8 Inch Mortar

a large carrying
a 18 pounder a side

an 8 Inch Howitzer

Battery of 18 Guns

a 13 Inch Mortar

The Vigilant carrying

Rebel floating Battery Galley &c.a

The only passage for Ships left by the Rebels

Isis

Roebuck

Earl

Somerset

British Ships of War!

Rebel Ba

Aaron Burr in Exile

Aaron Burr (1756–1836) kept a journal while living
in self-imposed exile for three years. The disgraced
politician, who had killed rival Alexander Hamilton
and been tried (and acquitted) for high treason,
fled America in 1808 to avoid public opprobrium and
mounting debts. On sheets of scruffy notepaper,
Burr jotted observations and encounters as he roamed
the cities of Europe. The lively, poignant account—
bound later into four volumes—indicates a man with
an insatiable appetite for money, gossip, sex, and
political schemes.

Self-Improvement

Benjamin Franklin (1706–1790), the famed polymath and prolific wit, began writing his memoir at age sixty-five. He spent nineteen years penning his life story in four distinct bursts, immodestly envisioning it as a guide in "moral Perfection" to instruct the young. Franklin listed the thirteen virtues on which he had attempted to model his life: temperance, silence, order, resolution, frugality, industry, sincerity, justice, moderation, cleanliness, tranquility, chastity, and humility. He added the last after a friend accused him of being proud. The document, the most extensive in Franklin's own hand, contains a mystery as well: a mishap nearly obliterated a page with a smear of brown ink. Franklin composed the last seven pages in the final two years of his life, and the narration ends midsentence. The autobiography, though unfinished, became a classic self-improvement guide. It has remained continuously in print for 225 years.

FACING
Benjamin Franklin, *Autobiography*
(detail), autograph manuscript,
1771–89, 13 ¾ x 9 ½ in. Purchased
by Henry E. Huntington, E. Dwight
Church Library, 1911

... Weeks ... say ... opened our Se...
our Press in Order ... fore Geo...
Acquaintance of mine, bro...
... us when he had me
... but enquiring for a Po...
... was now expen...
... Particulars
... I this Count...
... being in Te...
... ...ably, ya
... how ... Cours
... our own ... and has ...
... as ... ready, than po...
... not have been ...
... experience

... have mention...
... return of ...
... had form'd me
... Acquaintance
... for mutual Improvem...
... which we call the
... every Friday Eve...
... set up requir'd
... in his Turn some
... Queries on an...
... ther or Natura...
... to be discuss'd by the
... ... being once in th...
... because ... an expe... moderno ... and read a...
... upon any
...delphia was ... being on any
...ready half Bank ... Our Debates ...
... and all Appeara... Direction of
... new Buildings & the Rise of ...
... being to his certain Kno... conducted in
...ons, for they were infe... of Enquiry after Tr...
... things that I would soon ...
... gave me such a Deta... ...spects, or
... now existing or that ... ...preved th...
... that he left me half me...
... I known him before I cou...
... probably I should accompany ...
... have done it This Ne...
... to live in ...

Gothic Revival

The English writer John Ruskin (1819–1900) made this
sketch for a plate in his *Seven Lamps of Architecture*
(1849), a book that argues strenuously for an architectural
practice guided by ideals as well as the preeminence
of the Gothic Revival style. Ruskin's status as a widely
known public figure long ago waned, but in 1919, the
critic's role as a cultural arbiter remained unquestioned.
Here, Ruskin's sketch of the church of Nôtre-Dame in
Saint-Lô, France, underscores the superiority of Gothic
architecture because, like nature, it avoids strict symmetry.
The stylized acanthus leaves on the central triangular
pediment stretch and unfurl, much like the living weed
that has taken root on the left. Ruskin despised the
machine-made precision of nineteenth-century manufac-
tured goods, and the variation in his pencil marks—heavy
to light, rapid to refined—emphasizes the building's age
and hand-carved irregularities.

ABOVE AND FACING
John Ruskin, *The Seven Lamps
of Architecture* (1849),
(facing) "Façade of Cathedral of St.-Lô,
Normandy" (detail), 1840s, pencil
on vellum, 17 ½ x 12 ½ in. Purchased
by Henry E. Huntington, William K.
Bixby Library, 1918

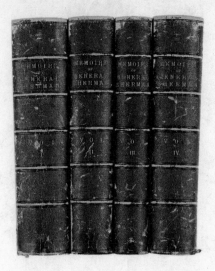

A General Remembers

Huntington focused much of his purchasing power
on original documents related to famed leaders of the
Civil War. William Tecumseh Sherman (1820–1891),
the Union Army general known for his "scorched-
earth" tactics, began his memoirs in 1872, seven years
after war's end. In them, Sherman vividly recalls
political maneuverings, numerous battles, and strat-
egies. Even so, more than a third of the manuscript
recounts other facets of Sherman's military career.
Memoirs of General William T. Sherman, published
in May 1875, was drawn from these four volumes of
reminiscences, dispatches, letters, and government
accounts. The book sold ten thousand copies in two
weeks and sparked controversy related to Sherman's
self-aggrandizing recollection of certain events.

4

missing.

...ss was heavy and occured chiefly at the point near ...Ricketts Battery was destroyed. Lt Col Haggarty was ...about noon, before we had effected a junction with Col ...s division. Col Cameron was mortally wounded ...his Regiment in the Charge. and Col Corcoran ...n missing since the Cavalry Charge near the Buil- ...sed as a Hospital;

	Killed	wounded	missing	Total
...ry	6	3	0	9
...th	11	29	20	58
...9°	38	59	95	192
...°	32	51	115	198
...°	24	65	63	152
	111	205	293	609

For names, Rank &c of the above, I refer to the ...ewith.

...s Piper & Mc Questen of my personal staff were under ...ll day and carried orders to and fro with as much ...s as on Parade, Lt Bagley of the N.Y. 69th a Volunteer ...asked leave to serve with his company during the ...and is among those reported Missing. I have intelli- ...that he is a prisoner. and slightly wounded.

...s Coon of Wisconsin a Volunteer Aid Also rendered ...rvice during the day.

W. T. Sherman
Col Comdg Brigade.

New York *Oct 18th 1919*

M *H. E. Huntington*

To **GEORGE D. SMITH**, Dr.

Old and Rare Books, Autographs, Prints Etc.

70 WALL STREET
Telephone 6942 Hanover

8 East 45th Street
~~547 FIFTH AVENUE~~
Telephone 2626 Murray Hill

*Collection of Revolutionary
Letters Washington Letters
Diaries etc.* — $16000—

*Recd Paymt
by ck Geod Smith*

New York April 16, 1919

M F. H. E. Huntington

To **GEORGE D. SMITH**, Dr.

Old and Rare Books, Autographs, Prints Etc.

~~70 WALL STREET~~
Telephone 6942 Hanover

8 East 45th Street
~~547 FIFTH AVENUE~~
Telephone 2626 Murray Hill

Dr. Johnson Autograph Letters, Ms. Portraits etc.
St. Augustin City of God 1467 Jones Copy
Kipling Ms. & volume illustrations etc.
Two Manuscripts, Hours and Brevarium $ 23000.00

Accepted Payable (10) Ten months after date. (February
16th, 1920)
                          H. E. HUNTINGTON,
                        BY

                        ATTY. IN FACT

Duplicate

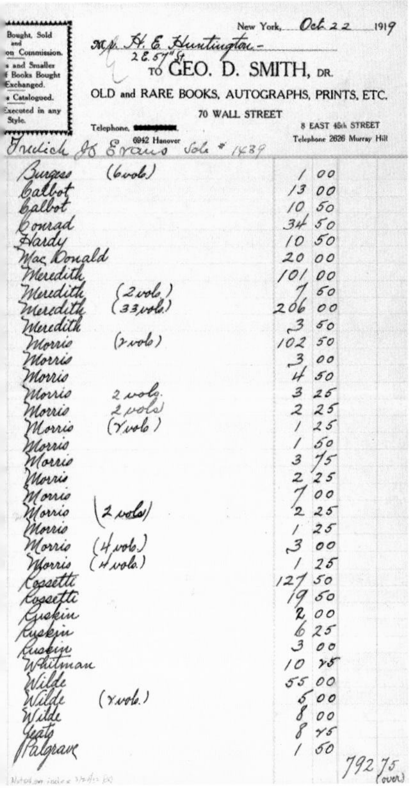

Bought, Sold and on Commission. Libraries and Smaller Parcels of Books Bought and Exchanged. Libraries Catalogued. Binding Executed in any Style.

New York, Oct 22 1919

Mr H. E. Huntington—
2 E. 57th St

TO GEO. D. SMITH, DR.

OLD and RARE BOOKS, AUTOGRAPHS, PRINTS, ETC.

70 WALL STREET

Telephone, [redacted] 6942 Hanover

8 EAST 45th STREET
Telephone 2626 Murray Hill

Fredrick JS Evans Sale # 1439

Burgess	(6 vols)	1 00
Calbot		13 00
Calbot		10 50
Conrad		34 50
Hardy		10 50
Mac Donald		20 00
Meredith		101 00
Meredith	(2 vols)	7 50
Meredith	(33 vols)	206 00
Meredith		3 50
Morris	(2 vols)	102 50
Morris		3 00
Morris		4 50
Morris	2 vols	3 25
Morris	2 vols	2 25
Morris	(2 vols)	1 25
Morris		1 50
Morris		3 75
Morris		2 25
Morris		7 00
Morris	(2 vols)	2 25
Morris		1 25
Morris	(4 vols)	3 00
Morris	(4 vols)	1 25
Rossetti		127 50
Rossetti		19 50
Ruskin		2 00
Ruskin		6 25
Ruskin		3 00
Whitman		10 75
Wilde		55 00
Wilde	(2 vols)	5 00
Wilde		8 00
Yeats		8 75
Palgrave		1 50
		792 75 (over)

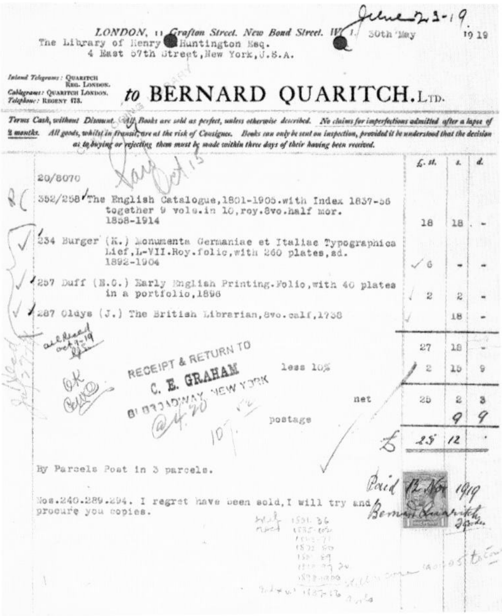

June 23-19.

LONDON, 11 Grafton Street. New Bond Street. W. 1. 30th May 1919

The Library of Henry E. Huntington Esq.
4 East 57th Street, New York, U.S.A.

Inland Telegrams: Quaritch Reg. London. Cablegrams: Quaritch London. Telephone: Regent 473.

to BERNARD QUARITCH. Ltd.

Terms Cash, without Discount. All Books are sold as perfect, unless otherwise described. No claims for imperfections admitted after a lapse of 2 months. All goods, whilst in transit, are at the risk of Consignee. Books can only be sent on inspection, provided it be understood that the decision as to buying or rejecting them must be made within three days of their having been received.

	£. st.	s.	d.
20/8070			
352/258 The English Catalogue, 1801-1905. with Index 1837-56 together 9 vols. in 10, roy. 8vo. half mor. 1858-1914	18	18	-
234 Burger (K.) Monumenta Germaniae et Italiae Typographica Lief, L-VII. Roy. folio, with 260 plates, sd. 1892-1904	6	-	-
257 Duff (E.G.) Early English Printing. Folio, with 40 plates in a portfolio, 1896	2	2	-
287 Oldys (J.) The British Librarian, 8vo. calf, 1738		18	-
	27	18	-
less 10%	2	15	9
net	25	2	3
postage		9	9
£	25	12	.

RECEIPT & RETURN TO
C. E. GRAHAM
61 BROADWAY, NEW YORK

all Recd Oct 9-19

By Parcels Post in 3 parcels.

Nos. 240. 289. 294. I regret have been sold, I will try and procure you copies.

Paid 12 Nov 1919
Bernard Quaritch

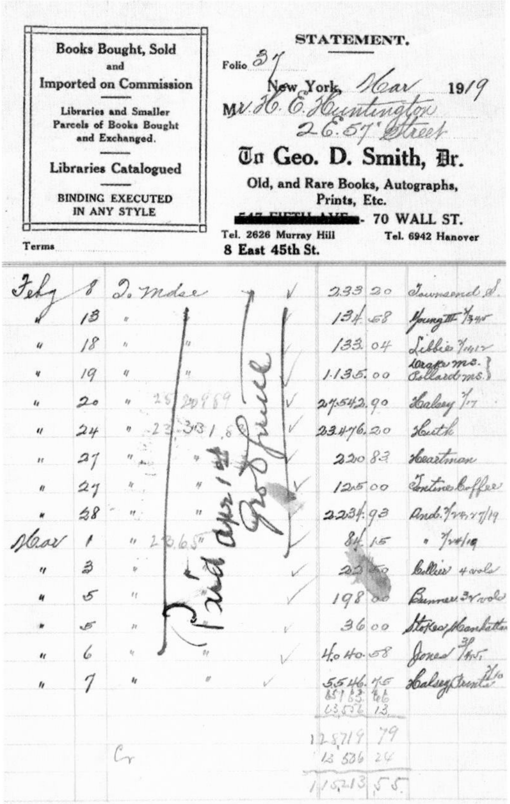

Books Bought, Sold and Imported on Commission

Libraries and Smaller Parcels of Books Bought and Exchanged.

Libraries Catalogued

BINDING EXECUTED IN ANY STYLE

STATEMENT.

Folio 37

New York, Mar 1919

Mr H. E. Huntington
2 E. 57th Street

To Geo. D. Smith, Dr.

Old, and Rare Books, Autographs, Prints, Etc.

[redacted] - 70 WALL ST.

Tel. 2626 Murray Hill
8 East 45th St.

Tel. 6942 Hanover

Terms

Feby	8	To Mdse	233 20	Townsend S.
"	13	"	134 58	Young
"	18	"	133 04	Libbie
"	19	"	1.135 00	Drake ms. Pollard ms.
"	20	"	27.542 90	Halsey
"	24	"	23.476 20	Huth
"	27	"	220 83	Heartman
"	27	"	125 00	Tontine Coffee
"	28	"	2.234 93	And.
Mar	1	"	84 15	"
"	3	"	22 50	Collier 4 vols
"	5	"	198 00	Bunner 3 vols
"	5	"	36 00	Stokes Manhattan
"	6	"	4.040 58	Jones
"	7	"	5.546 75	Halsey
			65163 66	
			63,556 13	
			128719 79	
		Cr	13 506 24	
			115213 55	

Paid Apr 1st
Geo D Smith

ABOVE AND FACING
Invoices and statements detailing Henry Huntington's library purchases, 1919

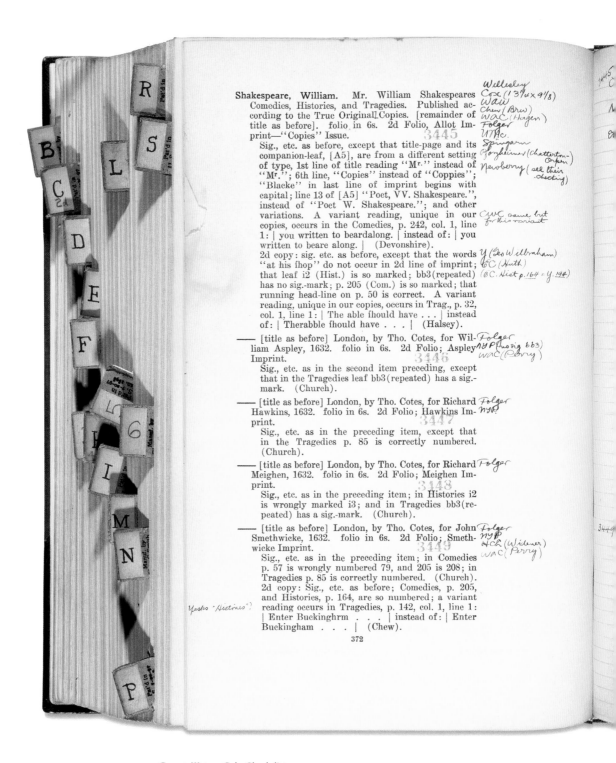

Shakespeare, William. Mr. William Shakespeares Comedies, Histories, and Tragedies. Published according to the True Original Copies. [remainder of title as before]. folio in 6s. 2d Folio, Allot Imprint—"Copies" Issue. 3445

Sig., etc. as before, except that title-page and its companion-leaf, [A5], are from a different setting of type, 1st line of title reading "M^{r.}" instead of "M^r."; 6th line, "Copies" instead of "Coppies"; "Blacke" in last line of imprint begins with capital; line 13 of [A5] "Poet, VV. Shakespeare.", instead of "Poet W. Shakespeare."; and other variations. A variant reading, unique in our copies, occurs in the Comedies, p. 242, col. 1, line 1: | you written to beardalong. | instead of: | you written to beare along. | (Devonshire).

2d copy: sig. etc. as before, except that the words "at his ſhop" do not occur in 2d line of imprint; that leaf i2 (Hist.) is so marked; bb3 (repeated) has no sig.-mark; p. 205 (Com.) is so marked; that running head-line on p. 50 is correct. A variant reading, unique in our copies, occurs in Trag., p. 32, col. 1, line 1: | The able ſhould have . . . | instead of: | Therabble ſhould have . . . | (Halsey).

—— [title as before] London, by Tho. Cotes, for William Aspley, 1632. folio in 6s. 2d Folio; Aspley Imprint. 3446

Sig., etc. as in the second item preceding, except that in the Tragedies leaf bb3 (repeated) has a sig.-mark. (Church).

—— [title as before] London, by Tho. Cotes, for Richard Hawkins, 1632. folio in 6s. 2d Folio; Hawkins Imprint. 3447

Sig., etc. as in the preceding item, except that in the Tragedies p. 85 is correctly numbered. (Church).

—— [title as before] London, by Tho. Cotes, for Richard Meighen, 1632. folio in 6s. 2d Folio; Meighen Imprint. 3448

Sig., etc. as in the preceding item; in Histories i2 is wrongly marked i3; and in Tragedies bb3 (repeated) has a sig.-mark. (Church).

—— [title as before] London, by Tho. Cotes, for John Smethwicke, 1632. folio in 6s. 2d Folio; Smethwicke Imprint. 3449

Sig., etc. as in the preceding item; in Comedies p. 57 is wrongly numbered 79, and 205 is 208; in Tragedies p. 85 is correctly numbered. (Church).

2d copy: Sig., etc. as before; Comedies, p. 205, and Histories, p. 164, are so numbered; a variant reading occurs in Tragedies, p. 142, col. 1, line 1: | Enter Buckinghrm . . . | instead of: | Enter Buckingham . . . | (Chew).

372

George Watson Cole, *Check-list or Brief Catalogue of the Library of Henry E. Huntington*, 1919, New York

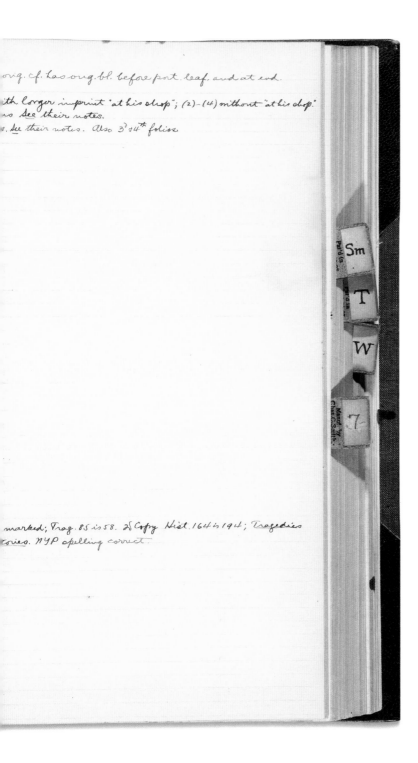

ong. cf. has ong. bl. before port. leaf. and at end.

ith longer imprint "at his shop"; (2)-(4) without "at his shop"
as See their notes.
s. See their notes. Also 3' 4th folios

marked; Trag. 85 is 58. 2d Copy Hist. 164 is 194; Tragedies
ories. NYP spelling correct.

In 1915, Henry Huntington hired seasoned bibliographer George Watson Cole to create a listing of all of Huntington's books printed prior to 1640. Cole considered the work ongoing despite these published results. This annotated copy belonged to Philip S. Goulding, one of the ten catalogers employed in the task.

Letters to be used in designating class of work:

A   Cataloguing (for new catalogue)
B   Revision
C   Writing old catalogue cards
D   Writing blue cards
E   Collating for duplicates
F   Copying cards
G   Listing and packing for auction room
H   Listing and packing for shipping
I   Unpacking and checking invoices
K   Making and checking lists for cataloguing-room

X   Other miscellaneous work (to be specified below)

FACING
G. Haven Bishop, *Interior of Huntington Library Building during Construction*, 1919–20, gelatin silver print, 10 x 8 in.

Report of Entire Staff for June 30–Sept 27 1919 (Third Quarter)

DAY	WORK	TITLES	VOLUMES	LEAVES	CARDS	TOTAL TIME
	A	178	118	21,379	927	766½
	B	205	137	22,865	925	181½
	C	562	542		996	143
	E	348	388			175½
Benditson	Miscellaneous					251
Bliss						313½
Denio	Bibl. Cat.					126½
Edmunds	References, etc.					308
Goulding	Check list					136½
"	Reports					18
"	Miscellaneous					12½
Knapp	Filing (o.c.)					99
Mead	" (1640)					8
Clapp	Miscellaneous					9
Schad	"					223½
	(Absences (cd 2)					27½
						63
	See next card				2835	(OVER)

Report of Entire Staff for November 10–15 1919

DAY	WORK	TITLES	VOLUMES	LEAVES	CARDS	TOTAL TIME
	A *	1	3		1	1*
	B	3		720	16	3½
	C **	583	645		1215	118**
	E	16	11			10
Benditson	Miscellaneous					38
Bliss						38
Denio	Bibl. Crit.					21
Edmonds	Critical Notes					38
Goulding	Check List					6
"	Reports					1
"	Miscellaneous					1
Knapp	Filing (o.c.)					10
Mead	" (1640)					½
Schad	Miscellaneous (Wendell)					38
Clapp	" readily					18
	9 @ 38 (1 hm. to Morgan Filing) →					342

* Denio revised one title
** Wendell Sale about the largest ever reported for the week, in all respects

(OVER)

Report of Entire Staff for June 30–September 27, 1919. Chief librarian George Watson Cole calculated the productivity and progress of each cataloger by title, volume, and page for Huntington's quarterly reports.

Gilbert Stuart, *George Washington*,
1819, oil on panel, 27 x 22 in.

*Huntington Residence under
Construction, South Wall in Dining
Room*, ca. 1910, glass plate negative,
10 x 8 in.

Head of State

Victorious leader of the Continental Army, president of the Constitutional Convention, and first president of the United States, George Washington was one of the celebrities of his age, representing a new republic that had tossed out the symbolism and regalia of the British monarchy. Savvy artists knew that money could be made from his portrait. One by Gilbert Stuart (1755–1828) is called an Athenaeum-type portrait, a replica of the one that was housed at Boston's Athenaeum (p. 219). This type is surely the most famous picture of Washington, appearing in reverse on the one-dollar bill. Busy running the affairs of the country and having already sat for Stuart once, Washington reluctantly agreed to sit for the portrait because Martha Washington, his wife, wanted a pair of portraits for Mount Vernon. The unfinished oil sketch served as a prototype for perhaps as many as ninety-two replicas made by Stuart. In 1919, Henry Huntington purchased one of the replicas for his library, along with one after Charles Willson Peale (1741–1827), one by Rembrandt Peale (not pictured), and another, less famous image by Charles Peale Polk (1767–1822).

ABOVE
Charles Peale Polk, *George Washington*, 1790–93, oil on canvas, 34 x 35 in.

FACING
After Charles Willson Peale, *George Washington*, after 1779, oil on canvas, 87 ½ x 51 in. Henry E. Huntington Bequest

Artist Charles Peale Polk begged George Washington to sit for a portrait. Polk pleaded in a letter that "not only will the desires of many Respectable Citizens be gratified; But the interests of a depending Family greatly promoted." It is not known whether Washington ever actually sat for him, but there are approximately twenty-eight copies of Polk's portrait, suggesting that he made money off of Washington's likeness one way or the other.

ABOVE
Calling cards for Henry E. Huntington.
Mr. Huntington probably used the
card with the black border—indicating
a person in mourning—after the death
of Arabella in 1924.

FACING
*Main Hall of Huntington Residence,
with Joshua Reynolds's "Jane Fleming,
Later Countess of Harrington" on
Display*, ca. 1928, gelatin silver print,
10 x 8 in.

Portraits

FACING
Henry E. Huntington under the Oaks at His San Marino Ranch (detail), ca. 1918, glass plate negative, 8 x 10 in.

PREVIOUS SPREADS
(pages 224–25) *Henry E. Huntington Visiting the Bird Refuge below the Cactus Garden on His San Marino Ranch*, ca. 1915, gelatin silver print

(pages 226–27) *Henry E. Huntington on the Grounds of His San Marino Ranch*, ca. 1919, glass plate negative, 8 x 10 in.

*Superintendent William Hertrich with a Tropical Tupidanthus
calyptratus on the Grounds of the San Marino Ranch*, ca. 1915,
gelatin silver print, 8½ x 6½ in.

Ranch

Henry Huntington announced a plan to retire from business in 1910, once he turned sixty years old. "I think I am entitled to some rest and playtime," he told the press. He fancied becoming a gentleman farmer on his 600-acre San Marino ranch.

Huntington had purchased the Southern California property in 1903 for the oddly exact price of $328,433.14. The ranch's former owner, James De Barth Shorb, had planted orchards, vineyards, and imported trees amid rugged canyons and native oaks but then went belly-up broke. Huntington planned to turn the agrarian paradise into a modern estate.

To make the acreage a self-sustaining farm, Huntington needed to make major improvements. William Hertrich supervised the upgrades he had in mind: a concrete stable, dairy barn, grain silo, milk house, and poultry yard with over a thousand birds. Six state-of-the-art greenhouses ensured fresh vegetables year-round.

In 1906, Huntington took a bite of an "alligator pear" while lunching at his Los Angeles club. Liking what he tasted, he asked the chef for some seed. He and Hertrich grew three hundred seedlings in pots, thus beginning the region's first commercial avocado orchard. Huntington liked to boast about this fact.

Hoping to discover other profitable varieties of fruit or tree to offset mounting costs, he expanded the ranch's citrus groves and cultivated thousands of plants from Mexico, Central and South America, and around the globe. The U.S. Department of Agriculture sent him persimmons, wine and table grapes, and additional varieties of avocado to plant and test.

The ranch's workforce proved equal to the owner's ambitions. Over a third of the eighty employees performed "general work." They had surnames such as Flores, Gutierrez, Sandoval, Morales, Lopez, and Hernandez, with each employee's payroll number preceded by "M," for Mexican, which translated to exactly thirty cents an hour in 1919.

Trees

Huntington loved trees. He sited his massive house next to two *Quercus engelmannii*, or native oaks. He had 650 mature specimens moved from nearby canyons and replanted all around the grounds.

A pair of giant trees that had collapsed years earlier pained him. Hoping to stave off further decay, the ranch superintendent performed a surgical experiment, filling the trees' cavities using steel and concrete. Huntington declared the operation a success.

A native New Yorker, Huntington was smitten with Southern California's many palms. He had large ones from around Los Angeles boxed and brought to the ranch. Each weighed from ten to twenty tons.

Two Canary Island date palms proved particularly close to his heart, having graced the garden of Collis and Arabella Huntington's home in San Francisco. After the 1906 earthquake and fire decimated their Nob Hill estate, he transported the fire-singed palms south, planting the pair in his new cactus garden. They became a living memorial to Uncle Collis.

Huntington also requested pepper trees, Himalayan cedars, and redwoods for the ranch. His superintendent installed fully grown camphors, deodar cedars, and a dammar pine at his boss's command.

On most mornings, Huntington wandered the grounds. He admired the oaks, the orange and avocado trees, the acacias and eucalyptus—his entire domain.

Superintendent

If Huntington had run a job advertisement for a ranch superintendent, it might have read something like this: "Wanted: experienced landscape gardener to transform rambling California property into magnificent country estate. No task too improbable or too small. Must live on-site. Must be available around-the-clock, seven days a week."

In 1904, William Hertrich, a twenty-six-year-old German immigrant, applied for such a job. Huntington's first directive? Make the gardens look mature. They should appear as if they had been in place for fifteen years, or more. He had a strict prohibition, too: no formal gardens allowed.

Hertrich went all in. He and his crew hauled dirt, graded land, built reservoirs, moved trees, and laid out roads. Gardens rolled out in rapid succession, with Hertrich tweaking and expanding the plan. "What about cactus?"

he suggested to a reluctant Huntington. It could be planted on an unsightly hillside where nothing else would grow.

Maybe a Mediterranean garden was too typical a choice, the superintendent hinted. Perhaps Huntington could consider planting cycads—the rarest of the rare—around the mansion instead? And what about propagating exotic seeds to see what would thrive?

The feverish construction decade was also the busiest of Huntington's professional life. Months would pass before he appeared on-site, but he insisted on weekly progress reports. "Don't forget to send me photographs," Huntington wrote. And so, the ranch superintendent mastered photography as well as everything else.

Hertrich indulged the owner's fancies and anticipated his whims. He worked out a complicated boiler system that piped heated water to the gardens, forcing winter blooms. He built a deer park, a turtle pond, glass houses for ferns and orchids, and an aviary for five hundred birds. He created a refuge for waterfowl, complete with a rustic bridge and an observation blind where Huntington spent his afternoons (pp. 224–25).

Many of Huntington's more ambitious plans clearly had Arabella in mind. She did not much care for California, but he hoped that an appeal to her horticultural interests would entice her to the ranch. In 1911, he told Hertrich to tidy a rock-and-bramble-filled canyon, and to be quick about it. A Japanese tea garden in Pasadena was for sale. The superintendent

William F. Hertrich, *Transplanting Large Cereus*, 1925, lantern slide, 4 x 3 ¼ in.

purchased its entire stock. He moved and installed trees, stone ornaments, plants, a bridge, and a house within fifteen months.

William Hertrich was a botanist, diplomat, fixer, visionary, and true lover of plants. He was a dream maker above all else.

In 1919, the payroll ledger listed Hertrich as employee number one.

Books

As a newlywed living in West Virginia in the early 1870s, Huntington started buying books in sets. He purchased collected works of history, poetry, literature, and criticism by and about leading British and American figures. Titles by Charles Dickens, John Ruskin, Isaac Disraeli, John Greenleaf

Whittier, and others added up to 108 volumes all told.

Those books became Huntington's collateral to buy out his business partner when their sawmill ran into financial problems in 1874. The loss of this first library caused him everlasting regret.

Huntington's book purchases eventually resumed when he moved to San Francisco and New York. He gravitated toward fancy bindings, books by iconic authors, and elaborate illustrated sets.

At first, he bought only English-language editions. He displayed an aversion, remembered one dealer, to books he could not read. That same merchant found it strange that Huntington never once inquired about price. Sophistication and discernment increased alongside experience and wealth. He came to rely on trusted dealers and professional librarians for advice.

In Huntington's suite of private rooms at the Metropolitan Club in New York, books were piled in every dusty corner and on every available seat. He prohibited routine cleaning around the tottering stacks, often taking his meals in that untidy lair.

In 1911, at a cost of $750,000 (the press erroneously reported the price as $1.2 million), Huntington acquired the E. Dwight Church Library en bloc. This single purchase, a famed assemblage of literary and historical gems, catapulted him from the ranks of rich book buyer into the ether of collector *extraordinaire*.

Huntington socialized with other bookmen and took companionable pride in sharing recent prizes. Like

Henry E. Huntington's New York Librarians, ca. 1919, gelatin silver print, 2 ¾ x 4 ¾ in. Seated (left to right): Philip S. Goulding, George Watson Cole, Herbert W. Denio, and Lodewyk Bendikson. Standing (left to right): Alan O. Whittaker, Leslie E. Bliss, Ralph J. Gifford, Robert O. Schad, Cecil K. Edmonds, Herman R. Mead, and Clifford B. Clapp. Not pictured: Chester M. Cate, who returned from military service in 1919

a child at Christmas, he eagerly opened and inspected the bundles and crates of books that arrived in an endless flow.

Afternoons in San Marino unfolded in the same way, Huntington sequestered in the library with its floor-to-ceiling bookcases and tapestry-lined walls. He made one thing clear: he was not to be disturbed. The bibliophile found pleasure and solace surrounded by his books.

Librarian

By 1915, Huntington knew that he needed professionals to catalog and track his growing inventory of more than 40,000 books. He insisted on one thing: all library employees must be men. He

hired seasoned bibliographer Dr. George Watson Cole to assemble a team. Leslie E. Bliss, a twenty-seven-year-old librarian, joined the initial staff, who were based in the Huntingtons' mansion on Fifth Avenue in New York.

Each day, Bliss scrambled up and down the stairs from the basement cataloging room to the library on the second floor (p. 196). Bronze bookcases flanked the long room, which reportedly "took away many a book lover's breath." He frequently encountered Huntington at his desk or stretched out in a chair, perusing a book. He described his employer as "somewhat shy and exceedingly gentlemanly."

A secret panel in the library concealed a safe that Huntington kept unlocked. He delighted in showing guests the treasures tucked inside: prized first editions of Shakespeare's plays, hand-written letters by Abraham Lincoln and George Washington, and, the pièce de résistance, a two-volume Gutenberg Bible that broke auction records when he paid $50,000 for it in 1911.

Bliss and his colleagues maintained a frantic pace. They checked the constant flow of acquisitions against dealer and auction lists, created catalog cards in an unconventional five-by-eight-inch size, and crated books for storage in California and New York. On occasion, Huntington strolled through this bibliographic beehive with a simple greeting and tip of his hat.

In 1919, Huntington announced a monumental move. He was taking his entire library west to California, and he wanted his New York librarians to come along. Most had considered their employment a prestigious, short-term job. Two quit immediately. Bliss and the remaining ten were, as Bliss recalled, "tickled pink."

Huntington appointed Bliss head librarian in 1926. He retired in 1958, after stewarding the collections for forty-three years.

House

Henry Huntington, often called "Edward," found contentment in family, nature, and books. In 1907, he hired the Pasadena firm of Myron Hunt and Elmer Grey to design the house of his dreams on the San Marino Ranch.

Huntington and Myron Hunt frequently met at the New York palace that Arabella Huntington called home. Edward was courting Belle, and he solicited her advice. She had overseen every detail of the majestic Fifth Avenue showplace where the three convened.

Hunt and Grey specialized in a Southern California idiom then in vogue, an architectural mash-up with elements from Italy and Spain, known as a Mediterranean style. The Huntingtons, the firm's wealthiest clients by far, had strong ideas of their own.

Belle argued for a big, imposing house, while Edward voiced more modest desires. Atop his list were a personal library and an outdoor room. Edward envisioned a capacious wicker- and plant-filled area with commanding mountain and valley views. It would be prototypically Californian, an indoor–outdoor space in which to read, relax, and entertain.

Hunt balked. The addition would be an unsightly appendage altering the residence's symmetrical plan, the architectural equivalent of the "tail wagging the dog." If Hunt could not fulfill the request, Huntington rebutted, another architect surely would. The loggia got built. It and the wood-paneled library became the largest rooms in the house.

The 60,000-square-foot Beaux-Arts mansion offered vast expanses to fill. Belle had spent three decades insatiably acquiring enough fine furnishings, paintings, and objets d'art to fill five mansions, plus one in Paris. Edward felt drawn to all things British; Belle was besotted by France.

In 1909, Belle reserved for Edward a suite of five Beauvais tapestries designed by François Boucher. The masterwork, begun in the late 1750s by order of King Louis XV, depicts aristocrats taking their ease in a bucolic setting of cupids, flowers, and pets. Titled *The Noble Pastoral*, it took a team of weavers nearly two years to complete. Edward paid $577,000 to acquire the set, far more than the cost of the house itself. The acquisition marked Edward's spectacular foray into fine art.

Belle continued to direct the purchase of sumptuous furnishings made for, and inspired by, French queens and kings. She also pointed Edward toward Grand Manner portraiture by British masters like Thomas Gainsborough, George Romney, and Sir Joshua Reynolds, an artistic genre he would go on to collect in depth.

A beaming Edward unveiled the house to Belle, now his new wife, in January 1914. He toured her through the airy, light-filled rooms, with their decorative furniture, jewel-toned rugs, and works of art shown to stately effect. A friend surreptitiously witnessed the private moment between the two. Edward appeared "radiant," he wrote, "thoroughly happy one of the only times in his life."

FOLLOWING SPREAD
Henry E. Huntington outside His San Marino Mansion, ca. 1919, glass plate negative, 8 x 10 in.

Loggia of Huntington San Marino Residence, ca. 1919,
gelatin silver print, 7 ¾ x 6 in.

Pets

Belle and Edward considered pets essential to a happy home. Two Angora kittens—one snow-white, the other jet-black—arrived with Edward at the ranch one day via private railcar from New York.

The felines joined a little fussed-over dog and three tropical birds. Mamie, an Australian cockatoo with a luxuriant yellow crest, lived in a tiled conservatory between the bedrooms upstairs. An affectionate Indian mynah bird made annual trips with the Huntingtons to the East Coast and back.

A saucy green parrot and the dog —both named Buster—had the run of the house. Buster the parrot was a real talker. On many an evening, he would cry out: "Edward, you're late. Come to bed! Hurry up! Hurry up!" This amused Edward to no end. Both Busters bit him whenever they could.

Buster the dog, a Brussels Griffon, was Belle's own pampered pet. He sat with her at meals and slept on her bed. One day, a ranch guard dog broke free, putting an end to Buster with a single ferocious bite. Belle ordered a tiny coffin made. She buried Buster in the rose garden and visited his grave every evening for months.

Arabella with a Beloved Cat, ca. 1903. Courtesy of The Hispanic Society of America, New York

Flowers

Belle insisted on flowers in extravagant displays.

Throughout her marriage to Collis, she cultivated roses, ferns, and exotic palms in custom-built greenhouses at their country estate. Belle taught herself horticulture, analyzing flowers under a microscope and studying botanical books. She became famed for specialty violets, which she grew by the thousands, scattering them around her mansions and giving them as gifts.

Edward had a cutting garden laid out at the San Marino Ranch to please her. Gardeners planted a carpet of 18,000 red tulips one season. A dizzying 30,000 yellow daffodils sprang up the following year.

But even the acres of gardens and grounds could not satisfy Belle's lavish tastes. Each day, local nurseries supplied fresh flowers—usually in blooms of red and white—and the staff arranged them in sprays of 50 to 200 stems to accommodate Belle's failing eyesight.

In one especially flowery year, an astonishing 34,000 blossoms came into the house.

Art Dealer

Archer Huntington, Arabella's son, described Sir Joseph Duveen as "the chief charmer of the picture business," a man whose "well-oiled courage knows no defeat." Archer's snide remarks notwithstanding, his acquisitive mother fell under the art merchant's spell. Duveen helped make his star client one of the most renowned collectors in the world.

The British-born Duveen worked for the eponymous family firm with galleries in London, New York, and Paris. Their winning tactic? Ferreting out treasures of European nobility for America's new nabob class.

The suave, silver-tongued dealer gained Belle's trust early on. Beginning in the 1870s, he helped furnish her New York mansions, each one more elaborate than the last. When she became a robber baron's widow in 1900, the spending really took off.

In 1906, Duveen purchased the Rodolphe Kann Collection of Old Master paintings and other priceless works. Belle cherry-picked two Rembrandts, including *Aristotle with a Bust of Homer*, and other precious objects from the lots. She reserved five eighteenth-century French tapestries for Edward, who was then courting her like mad. Edward paid more than half a million dollars for the set. He also hired Duveen to decorate his California house.

Duveen prided himself on incomparable customer service. For the Huntingtons, he hunted down superb Grand Manner British portraits that, with Belle's sly prodding, Edward began to collect.

Lord Duveen stayed as a guest at the San Marino mansion after Belle and Edward wed. He directed the exacting placement of paintings and furniture according to lighting and space. The smell of his cologne wafted through the house.

Both Huntingtons were "crazy about him," remembered their valet. They loved to hear him talk. Huntington the businessman valued the dealer's forthrightness about money and profit as well as his entrepreneurial skills. Belle gleefully bested Duveen at cards.

Duveen's cardinal maxim was, "When you pay high for the priceless, you're getting it cheap." The Huntingtons clearly agreed. Edward and Belle spent over twenty-one million dollars with the dealer in nine years, an average of over $6,000 a day.

Secretary

Carrie M. Campbell never left Belle's side. Family members and others described her as a secretary, a paid companion, and a good and faithful friend.

Known as "Miss Campbell," she was Belle's amanuensis, gatekeeper, and guide. She scheduled appointments, bargained with shopkeepers, wrote letters, signed checks. She read the newspaper aloud and took her mistress on

Henry E. Huntington and His Personal Secretary, Mr. Varnum, in the Rose Garden (detail), ca. 1918, gelatin silver print

Miss Carrie M. Campbell (left) *Traveling with Arabella Huntington in Europe*, ca. 1898. Courtesy of The Hispanic Society of America, New York

daily outings when Belle lost most of her sight.

Belle and Carrie were seven years apart in age. They met in 1870, when Carrie was fourteen. Belle and her baby, Archer, had left New York City to stay with the Campbell family in New Orleans. By the late 1880s, Miss Campbell had become Belle's indispensable assistant, traveling with her, Collis, and Archer on trip after trip.

Like both her Huntington husbands, Belle valued loyalty above all else. Immense wealth attracted all sorts of posers and hangers-on. Who better than a longtime intimate to keep one's secrets safe?

Miss Campbell never married, giving herself wholly to the Belle Cause. She worked for her mistress for thirty-five years. But when Belle died in 1924, Edward barred Miss Campbell from the Pasadena funeral, despite her decades-long, around-the-clock attention to his wife. No one knows why.

Valet

Alfonso C. Gomez scared the rest of the Huntington staff. The Spanish-born Gomez had once worked as a steward on a transatlantic cruise liner. As Huntington's valet and the household's majordomo, he ran a tight ship.

He awakened Huntington at eight o'clock sharp and kept him to a predictable routine: breakfast, bath, dress, mail, cards, lunch, and nap. By the time Gomez readied Huntington for bed at eleven each night, the valet had met his boss's every need.

Gomez admitted that Arabella was the "real master of the house."

She dressed for dinner in a black evening gown, sweeping down the grand staircase like a queen. In order to please her, "everything had to be *just so*."

Huntington had eccentricities, too. He insisted on fastidious grooming, especially of his flowing mustache. He stipulated that servants dress in blue. He required Gomez to sing a favorite barroom song to wake him up, even when the valet demurred. "Here's to good old whiskey," Gomez had to croon, "drink it down, drink it down!" Huntington relished a joke, sometimes at another's expense.

From 1911 onward, Huntington kept Gomez close at hand. The valet nursed him through illness, observed his personal relationships, listened in on business meetings, and served as confidante. Gomez saw the enigmatic Huntington weep "like a baby" two times: after the untimely death of Howard, his only son, from stomach cancer, and on the eve of his own death, in 1927.

On more than one occasion, Gomez heard his boss lament that he "had no friends."

Acknowledgments

A centennial exhibition inevitably takes stock and looks forward. The stakes are big. The pressure is real. This is especially so at an institution as august and mythic and complex as The Huntington. We learned this truth early on, and knew we needed to combine our complementary skills to take on the challenge. And what a mind-expanding, surprising, and humbling journey it has been. The single greatest perk—aside from being fully and happily immersed (sometimes literally up to our elbows) in The Huntington's extraordinary collections—was the collegial *esprit de corps* that made the process possible and pleasurable.

We owe huge thanks to the many, many Huntington colleagues across all divisions and departments who championed our efforts, facilitated our research, and assisted in countless, selfless ways. These include Karen R. Lawrence, President; the Huntington Senior Staff, especially Randy Shulman, Vice President for Advancement; Susan Turner-Lowe, Vice President for Communications and Marketing; Steve Hindle, W. M. Keck Foundation Director of Research; Sandra Brooke, Avery Director of the Library; Jim Folsom, Marge and Sherm Telleen/Marion and Earle Jorgensen Director of the Botanical Gardens; and Christina Nielsen, Hannah and Russel Kully Director of the Art Collections.

Certain members of the Exhibitions and Collections Management departments (aka Team Nineteen Nineteen) deserve special praise, particularly Lana Johnson, Sharon Robinson, Angela Fann, Jenny Werner, Erin Aitali, Erin Donovan, Susan Colletta, Valerie Flores, Ming Aguilar, and Lindsey Hansen. Curators across the three collecting divisions—Art, Botanical, and Library—proved characteristically generous with their time and expertise, including Peter Blodgett, Erin Chase, Claudia Funke, Catherine Hess, Joel A. Klein, Dan Lewis, Melinda McCurdy, David Mihaly, Kathy Musial, Karla Nielsen, Laura Rips, Natalie Russell, Krystle Satrum, Clay Stalls, Stephen Tabor, Tim Thibault, John Trager, Olga Tsapina, Vanessa Wilkie, and Li Wei Yang.

Several individuals and departments need to be singled out for efforts that were nothing short of heroic: Holly Moore, Jessamy Gloor, Christina O'Connell, Emily Lynch, Austin Plann Curley, Amanda Burr, Andrea Knowlton, and Kristi Westberg, Preservation; Kevin Miller, Mark Fleming, James Kitahara, and Samuel Wylie, Reader Services; Livia Hirsch-Shell and Dorothy Auyong, Acquisitions, Cataloging and Metadata Services; Sean Lahmeyer, Botanical Collections; Jerry Eaton, Facilities; Manuel Flores, John Sullivan, and Devonne Tice, Imaging Services; and for their superb research and fact-checking skills, we are indebted to Lily Allen (who also wrote several excellent object entries included in the text), Elvis Arteaga, Molly Curtis, Marianna Davison, Suzanne Oatey, and Anita Weaver.

Our scholarship and thinking benefited immensely from the intellectual generosity of various scholars, writers, and former colleagues, including the Rev. J. Edwin Bacon, jessie 'little doe' baird, Shelley M. Bennett, William Deverell, Gary Gallagher, Lynell George, Catherine Gudis, Alan Jutzi, José Luis Lazarte Luna, Perry Leavell, Paul Lerner, Natalia Molina, John O'Neill, Robert C. Ritchie, Martha A. Sandweiss, David Torres-Rouff, Judi Urquhart, Tiziana Venturi, and Joan Waugh. We also appreciate the wisdom and guidance of Kiara Boone and James Warren at the Equal Justice Initiative in Montgomery, Alabama.

Some excellent books on the year 1919 deeply informed this catalogue, including David Fromkin, *A Peace to End All Peace: The Fall of the Ottoman Empire and the Creation of the Modern Middle East*; Ann Hagedorn, *Savage Peace: Hope and Fear in America, 1919*; David F. Krugler, *1919, The Year of Racial Violence: How African Americans Fought Back*; Margaret MacMillan and Richard Holbrooke, *Paris 1919: Six Months That Changed the World*; and Cameron McWhirter, *Red Summer: The Summer of 1919 and the Awakening of Black America*.

To work on this project with the brilliant Kimberly Varella of Content Object Design Studio and her team, including MJ Balvanera, Lisa Doran, and Nikki Roach, has been a dream come true. Kimberly brought Ian Byers-Gamber to the project. He photographed some choice objects and made the series of site-specific images reproduced in the book. This volume would simply not have been possible without the prodigious work and singular grace of Jean Patterson, editor *extraordinaire*.

Finally, our gratitude goes to the funders who made this project possible: Avery and Andrew Barth, Terri and Jerry Kohl, Lisa and Tim Sloan, and the Gladys Krieble Delmas Foundation.

James Glisson
Interim Chief Curator of American Art

Jennifer A. Watts
Curator of Photography and Visual Culture

243

THE HUNTINGTON
Library, Art Collections, and Botanical Gardens

Published on the occasion of the exhibition
Nineteen Nineteen, organized by The
Huntington Library, Art Collections, and
Botanical Gardens, September 21, 2019–
January 20, 2020.

ISBN 978-0-87328-268-0

Printed and bound in China

Distributed by Angel City Press
2118 Wilshire Blvd. #880
Santa Monica, CA 90403-5784
www.angelcitypress.com
@AngelCityPress

The Huntington's Centennial Celebration is
made possible by the generous support of
Avery and Andrew Barth, Terri and Jerry Kohl,
and Lisa and Tim Sloan.

Support for this exhibition is provided by
the Gladys Krieble Delmas Foundation and
The Ahmanson Foundation Exhibition and
Education Endowment.

Project management
and copyediting—
Jean Patterson

Editorial and photo assistance—
Lindsey Hansen

Proofreading—
Ann Lucke

Art direction and design—
Kimberly Varella, Content Object

Principal photography—
John Sullivan and Manuel Flores,
Imaging Services

Color management—
Echelon Color

Printing and binding management—
Permanent Printing Limited, Hong Kong

Library of Congress
Cataloging-in-Publication Data

Names: Glisson, James, author. |
Watts, Jennifer A., author. | Henry E.
  Huntington Library and Art Gallery,
issuing body.
Title: Nineteen nineteen / James Glisson and
Jennifer A. Watts.
Description: San Marino, California :
  The Huntington Library, Art Collections, and
Botanical Gardens, [2019] |
"Published on the occasion of
  the exhibition Nineteen Nineteen, organized
by The Huntington Library, Art
  Collections, and Botanical Gardens,
September 21, 2019/January 20, 2020"—
  Copyright page.
Identifiers: LCCN 2019003936 | ISBN
9780873282680 (hardcover : alk. paper)

Subjects: LCSH: Nineteen nineteen, A.D.—
Exhibitions. | United
  States—History—1919-1933—Exhibitions. |
Huntington, Henry Edwards,
  1850-1927. | Henry E. Huntington Library and
Art Gallery—Catalogs. |
  United States—History—20th century—
Exhibitions.
Classification: LCC E784 .G55 2019 | DDC
973.91—dc23
LC record available at https://lccn.loc.
gov/2019003936

British Library
Cataloguing-in-Publication Data

A catalogue record for this book is available
from the British Library.

JAMES GLISSON is Interim Virginia
Steele Scott Chief Curator of American
Art and Bradford & Christine Mishler
Associate Curator of American Art at
The Huntington. Text on pp. 11-13, 21-32,
37, 61-70, 86, 101-8, 114, 131, 141-50,
154, 156, 181-84, 198, 200, 208, 221

JENNIFER A. WATTS is curator of
photography and visual culture at
The Huntington. Text on pp. 11-13, 18-19,
43-44, 46, 58-59, 89, 98-99, 119, 138-39,
161, 164, 170, 178-79, 186, 193-94, 197, 202,
205-6, 210, 231-41

LILY ALLEN is curatorial assistant in
American art at The Huntington. Text on
pp. 40, 73, 76, 90, 125

This book is typeset in Domaine Text and
Display, Prestige Elite, and Bau LF.

Cover illustrations: (front) *Henry E. Huntington*
(detail), 1871, tintype; (back) *Arabella
(Yarrington) Huntington as a Teenager* (detail),
ca. 1865, tintype. Courtesy of The Hispanic
Society of America

Endpapers: (front) Trust indenture establishing
the Henry E. Huntington Library and Art
Gallery (detail), August 30, 1919; (back) Oswald
Hornby Joseph Birley, *Arabella Huntington* and
Henry E. Huntington, 1924, oil on canvas, 50 x
40 in. each

Facing and following spreads: (page 245) Rare
Book Stacks, Huntington Library; (pages
246-47) Basement staircase and Old Vault,
Huntington Art Gallery; (pages 248-52) Rare
Book Stacks; (page 253) Vault door into Rare
Book Stacks; (pages 254-55) Manuscript card
catalog; (pages 256-57) Vouchers, Herbarium;
(pages 258-60) Large Library, Huntington Art
Gallery. Images © Ian Byers-Gamber. Images
on pages 112-15, 154, 155 (bottom), and 186 also
by Byers-Gamber.

Illustration Credits: p. 64: © artist or artist's
estate; p. 150, above: © Estate of Abraham
Walkowitz / Licensed by Zabriskie Gallery,
New York; pp. 152-53: © Estate of Peggy Bacon,
courtesy of Kraushaar Galleries, NY

Unless otherwise indicated, all objects and
photography are from The Huntington Library,
Art Collections, and Botanical Gardens.

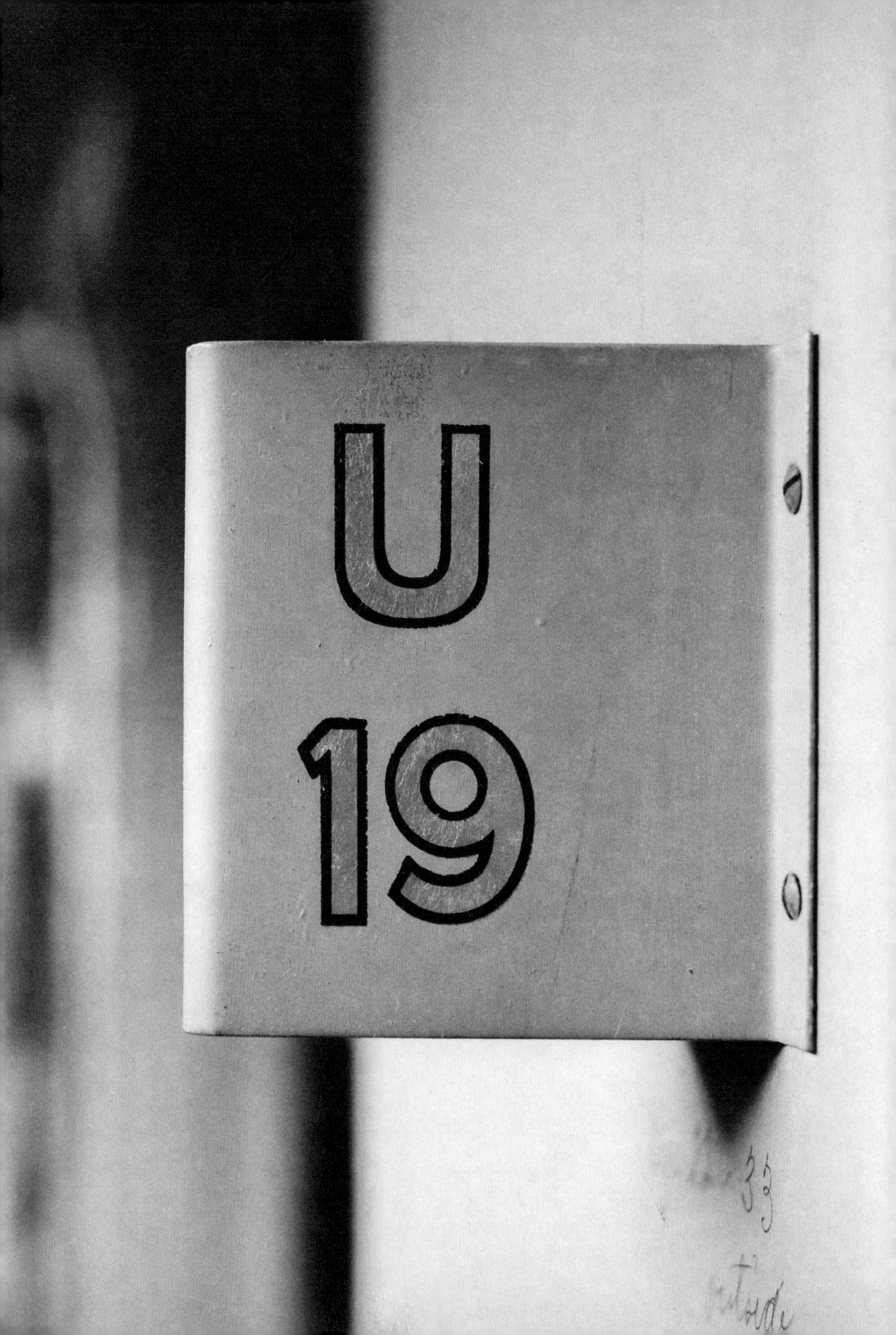
U
19

⑧ P411, P411A
P427, P427A

⑧ P428, P428A

⑧ P429 - P437

⑧ P37.5 - P440

⑧ P441 - P446.9

⑧ P447 - P452

BOX 9
FIJI
P498 - P507

BOX 9
FIJI
P508 - P515

BOX 9
NEW CALEDONIA
P516 - P523

BOX 9
NEW CALEDONIA
P524 - P529

BOX 10
New Caledonia, Java,
Malaysia: Pahang, Sarawak
P530 - P541

BOX 10
Malaysia: Pahang
P542 - P553

the heirs at law of said Henry E. Huntington.

All other personal property, including the contents of any building or buildings, library or art gallery, that may be constructed or erected upon said above described real property shall immediately pass to and vest in the Metropolitan Museum of Art, situated in New York City, New York.

IN WITNESS WHEREOF, the said grantors have hereunto set their hands and seals the day and year first above written.

Henry E Huntington (Seal)

Arabella D Huntington (Seal)

Subscribed, Sealed and
Delivered in Presence of:

_____

STATE OF CALIFORNIA,)
) ss.
County of Los Angeles.)

On this 12th day of September 1919, before me,

——— *J. E. Brown* ———, a Notary Public in